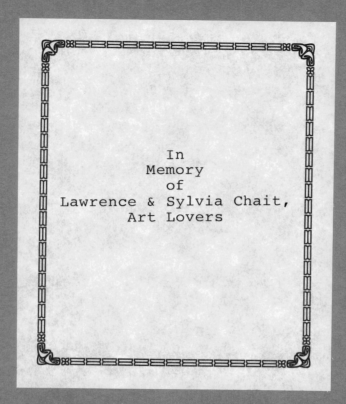

In
Memory
of
Lawrence & Sylvia Chait,
Art Lovers

SOTO:

A Retrospective Exhibition

THE SOLOMON R. GUGGENHEIM MUSEUM
NEW YORK

Published by The Solomon R. Guggenheim Foundation, New York, 1974
Library of Congress Card Catalogue Number: 74-16856
©The Solomon R. Guggenheim Foundation, 1974
Printed in the United States

Lenders to the Exhibition

Rosa Aguilera
Alfredo and Yolanda Boulton
Roger Boulton
Lya Imber de Coronil
William and Sylvia Ellis
José Hoffman
Milada S. Neumann, Caracas
Inocente Palacios
The Renault Co.
Jesús Rafael Soto
Dr. and Mrs. Carlos Raul Villanueva Collection,
    Caracas
José Rafael Viso

Kaiser Wilhelm Museum, Krefeld, Germany
Emanuel Hoffmann-Fondation, Kunstmusem Basel
Museo de Arte Moderno "Jesús Soto," Ciudad
    Bolivar, Venezuela
Museo de Bellas Artes, Caracas
Collection The Solomon R. Guggenheim Museum,
    New York

Galeria Conkright, Caracas
Galerie Denise René, Paris, New York
Galerie Françoise Mayer, Brussels
Marlborough Gallery Inc., New York

Acknowledgements

Soto's retrospective exhibition at the Guggenheim was selected from widely scattered sources. The largest share came from the artist's own collection at the Museum of Modern Art "Jesús Soto" in Ciudad Bolivar, Venezuela, as well as from private collections in Caracas, Paris and New York. Museums and private collectors were, without exception, ready to support Soto's first major museum show in the United States, and, as a result, responded generously to the Guggenheim's loan requests. We are, as always, grateful to lenders and list their names in recognition of their valued support. The catalogue also benefited from the added generosity of those who enriched its pages through donations for color plates.

Very special gratitude is due to Soto's principal dealer, Denise René, and his biographer, Alfredo Boulton. Both have followed the often complicated preparations with tolerance and generosity contributing time, effort and funds without which the show could not have been presented in its present format. Soto's own involvement, however, exceeds that of all others and the Guggenheim remains greatly in his debt.

These acknowledgements would remain incomplete were I not to mention the active cooperation of Renilde Hammacher-van den Brande, Chief Curator of Modern Art of the Museum Boymans-van Beuningen in Rotterdam, who encouraged and aided this project from the outset and who at a later stage was joined by Abram Lerner, Director of the Hirshhorn Museum and Sculpture Garden, Smithsonian Institution in Washington, D.C. These colleagues, who will probably be joined by others, will present the Soto exhibition in their own museums during the forthcoming season.

Museum staff particularly involved in the preparation of the exhibition and the catalogue includes among others Orrin H. Riley, Linda Konheim, Carol Fuerstein and Wendy Silverman at the Guggenheim Museum and Sergio Tosi of Milan and René Bleibtreu of Paris, the artist's friends and associates. We are grateful to all of these for their dedicated and sustained effort.

Thomas M. Messer, *Director*
The Solomon R. Guggenheim Museum

5

Preface

SOTO began as a painter and out of painting developed kinetic relief constructions which gradually grew into autonomous environments. In these, the spectator-turned-participant assumes a position so central that he is no longer divorceable from the work of art which without him remains incomplete. This process, traceable from phase to phase, took close to three decades of the artist's diligent and inventive life and gained for him an important place in post-war art.

As a student painter in Venezuela, where Soto was born, his first serious creative impetus came to him from a Cubist Braque still-life in a thrilling moment of comprehension, and his subsequent early work is an academic effort to learn from Cubism and from Cézanne the lessons of geometric simplification. When, as a youth of 27, Soto arrived in Paris, his avowed purpose was to find out what had happened in world art since Braque painted the still life that had so moved him. Proceeding from a sense of stylistic continuity, he shortly thereafter determined to put his own shoulder to the wheel at the point at which the art-historical carriage seemed to him to be stuck. Soto saw this point not in the then prevalent area of tachist expression (which he dismissed as irrelevant) but, rather, within an investigative tradition concerned with the object's position in time and space. He correctly traced the modern origins of this issue to Picasso's constructions, the researches of Gabo and Moholy-Nagy, the spatially suggestive paintings of Mondrian and Malevich and, more immediately, to the kinetic mobile art of Alexander Calder.

The young Venezuelan showed implicit faith in the logical progression of art. As a young investigator, but no longer student, he found himself attracted, together with Agam and Tinguely, to the orbit of the Salon des Réalités Nouvelles, established in Paris in 1946, and to the Galerie Denise René, which had opened its doors two years earlier. The group's patron-saint was Vasarely, and each of the young men in his own way embarked upon research having as its objective the visual representation of movement. By the mid-fifties, Soto and his friends had articulated their position and invented visual instruments for the expression of their principles.

Calder, as already mentioned, was the point of departure, but Soto's movement from the outset was different from that of the North American mobile maker. For Calder—the man who made sculpture move—did so mostly by letting carefully weighted, painted objects swing in the breeze, while Soto reduced physical motion to sensory vibration. The vibrating effect was either entirely based on optical responses to a physically static surface or further aided by the gentle movement of optically energetic suspended bodies as these came to act against similarly active optical surfaces. Leaving aside more distant antecedents, it may therefore be said that Soto related Calder's physical to Vasarely's optical kineticism, thereby combining palpable and visual kinetic elements into a new form-language.

The environments that Soto created, at the outset in experimental modesty, developed their own momentum and eventually spilled over from his visual laboratory into the world at large. His planes, initially created to reflect vibrations, gradually grew into a striated cube large enough to accommodate the traffic of crowds, and eventually came to dwarf and submerge man as he literally made his way through resisting but penetrable mazes. The prime experience in Soto's later works is no longer optical, but tactile and sonorous as the human participant, through his act of penetration, agitates not only the real space before him but also our aural ambience. (These sound structures, despite their importance in Soto's oeuvre, had to be omitted from this exhibition in deference to museum visitors who have come to see other displays in the building and whose right to silence we wished to respect.) Quite logically, Soto's most recent works are architectural. In his monumental factory interiors projected for Renault, the decorative and the structural elements of his kinetic idiom merge.

Soto's art, then, gradually develops from a sensory and contemplative to a physical, and in the case of the penetrable, to an athletic dimension; from the small laboratory experiment to monumental architectural scale; and from a self-contained aesthetic unity to one complementary to participatory activity by the viewer. Together with others, Soto has thus blurred the dividing line between the plastic and the performing arts; he has transformed the spectator outside the object to a central agent within the work itself; and reduced or radically altered the distance between art produced and consumed. Through these combined measures, for better or worse, Soto has greatly contributed to a perceptible shift away from art and toward life.

T.M.M.

Excerpts from an Interview

with Soto

by Claude-Louis Renard
Paris 1974

RENARD On the eve of your exhibition at the Guggenheim Museum, can you forget for a few minutes the fact that you are now an important artist and, looking back to your childhood and adolescence in Ciudad Bolivar, Venezuela, before World War II, recall your first contact with art?

SOTO My first encounter with art, professional art that is, took place in 1942, when I arrived in Caracas with a small scholarship to study at the Academy. But I never really had any other profession. When I finished primary school, I went to work as a commercial artist in Ciudad Bolivar, painting movie posters. I quickly established a modest reputation as a painter, which allowed me to apply for this scholarship to study in Caracas. Apart from this city, however, most of my childhood memories are of the landscapes and long years spent in the country.

C-LR You always continued to draw, after your first attempts. Was this a spontaneous need, a simple and direct pleasure, or was it already a reaction to other artists, even if by way of reproductions?

JRS No, there was no art at all in Ciudad Bolivar. I had never even seen an easel, for example. The first time I saw one was at the Academy in Caracas.

C-LR I've always been struck by the number of years during which you painted without any cultural references. You trained yourself, at the other end of the world, with no one to guide you.

JRS I wouldn't say that I had no one to guide me, since my old teachers at the Academy were artists, almost all autodidacts themselves and whose own training had come from art magazines and the few books which managed to reach Caracas. They were well aware of being unable to go any farther than Impressionism; they understood Cubism only vaguely, but they had the courage to show us the

8

few reproductions of Cubist works they had managed to find, somehow or other, usually in very mediocre art magazines. But I think these men liberated my spirit of experiment. Although incapable of it themselves, they always stimulated my gropings toward the unknown in art, instead of imposing upon me their own style of painting. I'm very grateful to them for this, and I'm always delighted, when I go back to Caracas, to see the few that are still alive; many are now dead, as they were quite old when they taught me.

C-LR What was the first work of art that you saw in Caracas which really impressed you?

JRS The work that made the deepest impression on me, when I arrived in Caracas, was a Cubist still life by Braque, placed on an easel. I was overwhelmed by this painting. It may seem strange, coming from Ciudad Bolívar, that I was attracted by this particular work, instead of being interested in descriptive or other kinds of art.

I asked artists and the more advanced students for information about the Braque and explored with them the reasons why this work interested me, and why, in a sense, it had been placed so prominently in the entrance hall of the Academy. They were very honest, telling me that I couldn't possibly understand a work like this immediately, that this was difficult art which had to be studied seriously to be absorbed in depth. So I worked hard studying and analyzing it, and by the end of my first year, I already understood Cubism and the more recent experiments by Picasso.

C-LR At an early age, you displayed that ferocious desire to understand, to go back to the source, which is deeply ingrained in you and which you've never lost, along with an attraction to whatever is new.

JRS Yes, my curiousity was all the more intense since, coming from Ciudad Bolívar, I had no general knowledge of art. I had seen reproductions of Millet's *Angelus* and certainly some color reproductions of Murillo Madonnas which I did not like enormously. Even as I listen to you, I'm surprised myself by my interest in Cubism then, as opposed to figurative art. I immediately set out to discover the sources of Braque's work, and through studying him, I began to understand Picasso. Then, on going farther back, I discovered the works of Cézanne and van Gogh. I was somewhat attracted to Gauguin, at a certain point, but I never was entirely convinced by his forms or his symbolic vision; despite these reservations, I loved his color. Later on, when I saw the paintings themselves in Paris, I was very disappointed, as these same colors seemed so dull. So much for my earliest memories of the Academy.

C-LR Were there any study materials available in Caracas —reproductions, art magazines?

JRS There were only a few reproductions available, a small library which had some art historical material up to Impressionism. Much later on, a few books arrived on Cubism and Fauvism, but by then, I had finished my studies.

C-LR Were you able, at this period, to see any actual paintings by these artists?

JRS During my last year there, I visited a private collection which contained, among other works, paintings by Sisley and Dunoyer de Segonzac. Here, for the first time, I saw paintings by real painters. But living in Venezuela, I couldn't really understand Impressionism, since the light in Impressionist paintings doesn't correspond to tropical light, which is very strong and bright. I was truly awestruck when I arrived for the first time on the outskirts of Paris. It was the beginning of autumn, and when I saw the russet birch trees, I immediately understood why the Impressionists painted as they did.

9

C-LR While you were finishing your studies in Caracas, did you continue to draw and paint for yourself?

JRS Yes, and then I went back to Ciudad Bolivar, where I was to have been a teacher, since I was given a stipend on that understanding, but they did not want me. Instead, I was asked to direct the small Academy of Fine Arts in Maracaibo, where I turned out to be the most diligent student. I painted as much as I could, day and night. I never did manage to convince my students to follow my example and work seriously, with the exception of one young woman who went on to become a painter and who, today, is the soul of Maracaibo. She never lost her zeal and converted the city to modern art.

C-LR What kind of painting were you doing in Maracaibo, at this point.

JRS I was trying to work at painting with Cubism as my point of departure, but it became obvious that, with no knowledge of what followed this movement, I was held back by ignorance. I knew that Cubism had developed at the time of the First World War, so I was obliged to guess what had happened between that period and the years 1948-50. I realized that much exciting activity must have taken place about which I was totally ignorant. I decided there was no point in trying to discover what had probably already been discovered, or in solving problems already solved . . .

C-LR . . . In recalling your beginnings in art, you naturally emphasize two fundamental qualities in your character which I've often observed in the course of our own collaborative projects integrating art and architecture within the last two years: first, a complete lack of interest in areas already explored, and conversely, a relentless determination to explore unknown terrain. Further, a consciousness, even if unformulated, of the immense labor involved in bringing these experiments to fruition with an austere economy of means, an assiduous avoidance of dilletantism, a very keen sense of what is essential and what isn't, in order to assure, in your own view, your creative survival. In essence, then, the evidence that something was happening in Europe which eluded you, was intolerable, becoming the main reason, I imagine, behind your decision to move to Paris.

JRS This was the only reason. I went where I thought I would find the raw material which had previously been inaccesible to me. And indeed, I quickly caught up and got to work on small personal studies in abstract art.

C-LR In the period before you left Venezuela, what sort of life did you lead? You painted and drew constantly, but had you already become involved with music? Were you living as you do now, or differently?

JRS No, I was living the same kind of life, and the friends who knew me then maintain that I haven't changed in the least, either in terms of my relationship with others or myself.

I still love music, and live a very casual life, seeing friends often; if I have any excuse to give a party, I give one. I don't, however, confuse my spontaneous impulses and my need to construct an art which is wholly rational; these are two things which I have never wanted to become confused. Many people have found a musical influence in my work. It's quite possible that it's there, but not in the sense of the popular music that I play; more in the direction of Bach, in the structure that my work reveals. But I see no reason why a man who is working very specifically in one direction can't also develop in others.

C-LR I feel that behind Soto, the man who one sees living from day to day, enjoying himself at a party, playing the guitar, talking to friends, taking a walk, sitting in a cafe, there is a secretive man—not hidden, in the narrow sense of the word, but self-protective, a man who has hiding places; a two-hour nap, a quick flight to change countries, isolating himself in a corner and letting others talk, even abstracting himself from a context he enjoys, in order to inexorably return to his work. Do you see yourself in this description?

JRS Yes, whatever the circumstances, even in the midst of a party, if there is someone really interested or interesting in the field of art, as I conceive it, I forget everything and drop everything to go back to work, because finally, that's what counts the most for me. I don't say that the rest doesn't matter, but the possibility of pushing farther ahead in my work is what constantly sustains me. If my vocation had been that of a scientist, I would probably do the same thing; conduct my research on an essentially speculative level.

C-LR This determination certainly helped you to acquire your own broad and highly individual culture, not at all bookish or theoretical, but highly selective, one which submits everything, without exception, to hard scrutiny. One has the impression that, behind the sensitivity of your approach, a critical intelligence is constantly on the alert. With every artist, you head straight for the essential questions: What was his contribution? Has he advanced, be it in the smallest degree, the history of art? Or has he merely repeated the discoveries of others? Is he a follower or is he really a force for progress.

JRS Yes, because without moving forward, there is no creation. Otherwise, one remains a primitive. If an artist isn't really a professional, if he doesn't conceive of art as a bulwark of culture, he should stay in Ciudad Bolivar and make primitive art, like everyone else, like many artists all over the world. Primitive art is certainly one form of expression, but in essence, it adds nothing; it always and everywhere remains the same. It's a valid evidence of human sensibility, but one having no bearing on cultural evolution.

C-LR In this area, how would you define the new, as opposed to what you call repetition?

JRS It's very simple. The real history of art, insofar as it has any meaning and interest for me, obviously isn't my invention, but has already been defined by innumerable creators and thinkers; like a wall which is built by the superposition and additions of cumulative contributions. Other parallel possibilities, meanwhile, always exist which may serve as stimuli to the creators, but most important for the history of art is the continuity of its evolution. This is a highly positivist view, but I believe that art should be positivist, that it should contribute to the education of society on a very professional level; since, as artists, we have been formed by Western culture, our art should evolve with the same seriousness as philosophy, mathematics and scientific research. For me, art is valuable when this evolution is rationally justified . . .

C-LR You left Venezuela, arriving in Paris in 1950. What did you find? South Americans, of course, and other friends. I don't see you ever leading a solitary life.

JRS Quite the reverse. A group of my friends had left for Paris the year before I did. I wrote to them and they were waiting for me with open arms. Through them, I quickly caught up. I borrowed all their books, and, with the help of a dictionary, worked until 5 A.M. every morning translating them, as I didn't know a word of French. Three months later, I had read nearly all the books and had gleaned all the available information. I next got in touch with the annual salon, Realités Nouvelles and with all the artists known to them at the time. By then, I had met all the artists in the Denise René circle who, at that point, were making, I felt, the real discoveries. I talked with these artists at great length. Then I went off to look at the work of Mondrian and Malevich.

C-LR Where did you see their work?

JRS I had thought I would find works by these artists in Paris, but there weren't any. So I had to go to Holland.

C-LR At the Stedelijk Museum in Amsterdam and the Kroller-Müller Museum in Otterloo?

JRS Precisely.

C-LR There certainly couldn't have been many books available on these artists.

JRS No, there were only a few articles: then the first book on Moholy-Nagy appeared in English in 1954. I bought it and found a kind and cultivated woman who generously translated two or three pages a night for me, until I had read the entire book.

C-LR Once again, I have to admire the way you educated yourself, step by step, like a craftsman, constantly checking the quality of his materials and tools, but without seeming to do so, letting others think of you as easygoing, living from day to day; whereas the truth is that your superficial nonchalance conceals an intense effort to discover, at whatever cost, every element necessary to the search for your particular mode of being.

JRS I do this consciously. I've always had the need to feel sure of what I possess. Mistakes don't matter to me. Not that I try to make mistakes, but I've always tried to make sure that what little I possess, I possess solidly enough to keep on going. I know that today, for example, I have had an experience that belongs to me, that I'm in secure possession of it: this makes it possible for me to continue working. But even had I not enjoyed a certain measure of success, I would have persisted in the same method of work. I don't think, in any case, that I could have been deflected.

C-LR In actual fact, you only became known, beyond the circle of your friends, around 1960, after the Venice Biennale, despite the fact that in 1955 you partici- pated in Denise René's exhibition Le Mouvement; this exhibition brought together for the first time the principal artists working in a direction similar to your own. Prior to that time, your reputation was underground. You were working in the dark, so to speak. But you still remained in Paris, when you might very well have decided to live elsewhere. Were you happy?

JRS Yes, very happy.

C-LR What were your primary interests, at this time?

JRS One incident had a profound effect upon me: a girl from Maracaibo spoke very contemptuously about the painting White on White by Malevich, in the Museum of Modern Art in New York, which has be- come, for me, a kind of spiritual touchstone. Then, on coming to Paris, I saw reproductions of several works by Kandinsky which had just begun to be published. I don't much like the Expressionist Kandinsky, but I do admire the highly Constructivist Kandinsky of the Bauhaus Period. I was also intro- duced to the work of Sophie Taeuber, I met Arp, and with these new influences, engaged in long discussions with other artists, especially my Latin- American compatriots, whose number and im- portance are both very large. The spirit of Bauhaus art attracted me particularly, along with those works by Klee which investigated perspective from several points of view. That interested me enormously. Obviously, I am leaving aside the symbolic aspect of Klee's art, but when he is most profound, in my view, his art is like a cathedral. With some difficulty I also discovered the work of Albers, since there were very few to be seen in Paris. But I found out as much about him as I could, and finally I saw his paintings thanks to Denise René who decided to put on a loan exhibition. The artists I remember most vividly from this period were Mondrian, Malevich, Klee, Albers and those friends with whom I discussed the exhibition.

C-LR What developments were taking place in your own work, during the period following your arrival in Paris.

JRS In the first period, after my arrival, I wanted to "dynamize" those works by Mondrian that meant most to me, since I decided the problem was one of giving them movement. I don't know, that was just my particular intuition. This was before I had seen *Broadway Boogie Woogie,* at which point I realized that Mondrian had already resolved this problem himself.

C-LR You were really reacting in the same way that you had towards the Cubists: the experiment had already been done, the solution found, and there was no point in wasting your time by repeating it.

JRS Yes, it had already been done, so I had to forge ahead. Thus, I began to explore in several directions. I found the discoveries of Moholy-Nagy very important, if incomplete, due to his premature death. But he was one of the most gifted artists of this period. I also discovered Calder, Marcel Duchamp and Gabo. Based upon the work of these artists, I began to construct a world, telling myself that I must make use of all the elements they had set forth, but whose implications they had not fully explored. I decided to try and find answers to all the questions they had asked, but left unanswered, what we call, in Spanish, *planteamintos.*

C-LR Questions left hanging? You emerge once more as a researcher.

JRS Yes, I set out to resolve those problems left unsolved by other artists, and I finally discovered what my real work was to become. I understood that there was something here that belonged to me alone. I began to develop my own direction, while retaining my respect for the artists who had guided me.

C-LR Would you agree that the first works which formulated these experiments in concrete form were the *Repetitions* of 1951?

JRS Yes, repetition possesses a universal character, revealing pure structure: that was a fundamental concept.

14

C-LR In this work, one already feels the disindividualization which is the source of all your later work.

JRS In order to create a truly abstract art—and when I say "abstract" I am using the word in every sense—one has to de-personalize; the individual no longer counts. To develop in my personal life, I prefer to get together with friends, give parties together, but I don't want to give my work any direct individual content.

C-LR It would seem that the richness of your personal life exists only to provide the most auspicious conditions for your work; ultimately it is your work, regardless of everything else, which orders your life.

JRS Yes, even vacations are work holidays for me. I can't seem to relax completely on a beach, like everyone else. It just isn't possible for me to do that. Stretching out on a beach for even an hour and forgetting the world is time lost for me. I love the sun, but I'm always thinking about work in progress.

C-LR How many times have you told me, while we were working on the project for the new Renault buildings: "Formulate the problem again, so I can ponder it while I'm travelling." Then, when you come back, having done all kinds of things on your trip, the solution has been found. You've been working all the time, without any real interruption. . . .
      Repetition is the first step in depersonalization, the first form of disindividualization, "disanimation," as you put it, but then you have to utilize the progression underlying this method.

JRS Repetition is an abstract value, perfectly inscribed upon the universal.
      Progression is a variation of repetition, but with a value which is not absolute; it is a point of departure. In order to universalize it, we have to conceive of a cyclical progression, where the point of departure loses its particular value.

Then, quite independently, I began reading books on serial music. I've always had a great admiration for the organization of a fabulous world made from simple and abstract elements, such as the world of Bach. By the same token, I was greatly impressed to discover that by using the series, one could construct a new world. So, around 1953, to resolve my own set of problems, I tried to codify basic colors in order to establish a serial system. Sometimes I'm asked why I didn't continue doing "serial" works. Simply because these serial works quickly led me to a new phase—the vibrating forms which became the goal of my subsequent experiments.

C-LR One period of your work was over: you had found what you were looking for, starting from *Repetitions,* moving to *Progressions,* then to the serial works. . . .
      I agree with you that this is not the place for a theoretical analysis of your development; rather, we are trying to give the public the background information necessary to allow them to place your work, both in the context of your life, and in relationship to the work of your contemporaries, or those among them whom you feel to be important. Can you, nonetheless, distinguish, from the point of your first vibratory works on, the major steps in your development?

JRS The serial works which followed upon *Repetitions* led to an optical vibration of the painting. From there, I moved almost immediately to the superposition of two vibrations, two repetitions, and superimposed progressions. And from this superposition, I arrived at optical movement through the displacement of the spectator in front of the stationary work. First came paintings like *Metamorphosis,* exhibited at Realités Nouvelles in 1954, with a shifted grid, where the question of time is interjected. Then I made *The Little Villanueva Box,* with its three transparent plaques, in which the entire surface is striated, with the exception of one unlined square on each plaque: this created a sense of ambiguous space, as well as optical movement. From there, I moved to the

15

Spiral and other works using plexiglas. I worked terribly hard on the problem of the presence of time in art; how to render it perceptible: here I had discovered an element which had to be developed. At this point, I made countless works in plexiglas, many of which are now lost. Gradually, I began suspending certain elements between the plexiglas and the opaque background, both of them striated. It became obvious that their movement could be integrated with optical vibrations: I then began to use these suspended objects which you know; "immaterial curves," rods, etc. . . . which, through the phenomenon of displacement, disappear, to be perceived merely as vibrations.

C-LR From the moment of your first use of plexiglas, it became apparent that the work of art, as you conceived it, although beginning as your own creation, could not exist without the active participation of the spectator, who, by his movements, causes the vibrations which you have set up. In all the works which followed, you constantly require of the spectator this participatory role which, like disindividualization and universalization, was, from this point on, integral to your art.

JRS I kept working in this direction for nearly two years, during which I discovered the infinity of possibilities offered by the superposition of two hatched surfaces. I was conscious of trying to discover values with which to construct something else later on, but I wasn't yet in control of the elements involved; as yet, they remained almost too free.

C-LR Were you in the process of mastering something new?

JRS That's just it. At a given point, I understood that I had to eliminate one of two liberties, and through this discovery, in 1957, I retained, almost mechanically, the tightly ruled background screen, leaving the superimposed element free. I then began to develop in that almost baroque sense you mentioned, using

16

a wide variety of materials, in order to prove that all elements were valid for my purpose. Once I understood that everything was possible, I once again began to control these elements, choosing the simplest ones, and those best suited to my experiments.

C-LR To translate this universality, you used the simplest materials, with an insistence upon economy and efficiency which has always characterized your work.

JRS Well, you know, I come from Venezuela, a country which, when I was growing up, was still undeveloped; to get anything done, you had to do it yourself. As I told you, I was looking for the moment when I would find exactly what I wanted, and, little by little, through my work, I acquired the vocabulary which allowed me to articulate my discoveries.

C-LR In all the retrospective exhibitions that I've seen of your work in Europe, I've always been struck by the evidence of a really miraculous success, all the more miraculous in that it has been repeated several times, but in an entirely new idiom each time, through different series of your work: this success consists in having found for each problem, the most pure and direct solution, by rendering the most simple elements capable of transmitting precisely those phenomena that you have isolated and made perceptible.

JRS I intend to keep working until I succeed in this, because I am indeed insistent upon economy of means.

C-LR For me, the works that you did between 1962 and 1967, Immaterial Curves, with their identical horizontal metal rods suspended on nylon wires in front of a uniformly hatched surface, Vibrating Squares, Suspended Parallel Rods, and more recently, the T's, stand as milestones in the stages of your development, now reaching definitive perfection. Still later, we find that same quality—precision of vocabulary—in those works which take shape in a much larger space, be they Penetrables, Extensions or Progressions on the Ground—works done after 1968.

Certain of your works, in terms of my own preferences, occupy a place apart; I have a special feeling for the series you call Writings. In one sense, I think they can be read as a very definite return to the direct line traced by the artist's hand, and while also remaining a coherent element in your goal of disindividualization, these exist as a more immediate transcription of your personal sensibility, as though you have allowed your hand, more or less consciously, to act with greater freedom. This is a rather mysterious region, rediscovered each time, as though we were observing too-intimate a process, in relation to the rest of your work.

JRS That's possible. For me, the Writings are a way of drawing in space.

Cruz-Diaz, one of my teachers, referring to an early version of Writings, said: "This is your language; the same signs you were making when you were trying to go beyond Mondrian." And it was true. I just had never thought of it that way. I was using the same curves I had used in drawing my early landscapes. Had I been a painter in the 18th century, it's perfectly possible that instinctively, my hand would have drawn the same lines. Perhaps . . . but even within this freedom, I still continue, you see, to retain a structure and to control the elements within it. . . .

C-LR It seems as though the displacement between the impersonal hatched screen of the background and the rods—folded or bent, as you freely decided—made it possible for you to create a language capable of expressing the maximum individuality compatible with your goal of universality. Even in the Writings, pure vibrations are never absent, but emanate from the vertical rods punctuating the rhythm of curved and broken lines.

In any case, these furtive incursions of a hand which do not, however, translate your "statement" are rare, and never lead you away from the real domain of your art.

JRS No, I have always continued to work in the same direction, and the Writings appear intermittently between my more rigorous and controlled experiments.

C-LR What was your reaction to the work of artists who have chosen directions entirely different from your own? Did you follow their work closely?

It is certainly characteristic of our time that explorations which seem radically opposed, taking place each within its own distant orbit, can co-exist, each following its particular trajectory without interference. Thus, as you come closer to achieving de-personalization and universality through a revelation of primal matter, other artists, conversely, are resolutely refusing any loss of individuality. Dubuffet, for example, is fiercely determined to seize the writhing of organized life, as it exists, from its most undetermined level to the abrupt outpourings of the imagination.

JRS Yes, that's a direction totally different from my own, but I certainly respect it. . . .

C-LR . . . Coming back to your work of 1968, you began to set limits, following a succession of experiments, to the terrain of your explorations. You gave the most concrete form possible to those preoccupations which had concerned you for more than 15 years. You have become the author of a coherent body of work which already occupies an important place in the evolution of contemporary art. It seems, nonetheless, that the years 1968 and 1969 represent an important turning point for you, in terms of three factors: first, your financial means have nothing in common with those of your beginnings and allow you more freedom to realize works on a much grander scale, like *Cube with Ambiguous Space,* or the long alignments—straight or curved—of vertical rods of the same dimensions as the room in which they are placed. The emphasis shifts to the relationship of the work to the spectator, and thus changes in nature: previously, the spectator had participated in the work merely by confronting it; now this same spectator becomes one with the space you have established. This revolutionary contribution is brilliantly formulated in *Penetrables,* where the spectator is placed in the midst of wires or vertical rods which have invaded all the available volume and which actually *are* the work, animating both spectator and work of art, now inextricably and physically joined. With *Penetrables,* you succeed completely in materializing your profound feeling of man in his situation, plunged into a "full" universe where space, time and matter become one, in a continuum of infinite vibrations. Finally—and this is undoubtedly the most concrete expression of this stage of your development—you now give a preponderant place to works integrating architecture, removing your art from its specialized locus, and joining it directly to the daily life of your contemporaries. This determination to make your discoveries available to others leads you to accept the constraints inherent in these recent integrated forms, that is, your own concepts must now function within a framework conceived by men who are often far behind in relation to the work you are doing.

JRS I accept these constraints. I don't see this as time wasted, since the work is deeply significant for me. I see no reason to refuse to adapt myself to a situation, such as it exists. I began my own work, unfortunately, when these other projects were well under way, since our society is still fixed at a certain concept of work. Mine is a supplementary effort. I calmly await the models and do what I can to intervene with the fewest possible compromises. I believe that the people who will pass through the new entrance hall of the Renault building every day, for example, between the screened pillars, the blocks of vibrating squares and the large *Writing* over 90 feet long which are unified by the ceiling made up of 250,000 rods suspended above their heads, will discover something within themselves of which they were not aware. . . .

Penetrables, the new works placed on the floor, the integrations with the architecture, are, in essence, the result of all my earlier experiments. I have always worked in the spirit of a researcher wanting to make a discovery; just as my serial works led to the

optical vibration of the painting, the superposition of works one upon another towards real movement, the explorations in the direction of a new language, model phrases, demonstrative elements, all led me towards pure abstraction. With my particular idea of the universal, there are no further limits: In principle, I could create a work which would stretch from Paris to Le Havre, or which would span the ocean—it would be the same process. Simply put, for a long while, I was only able to create small, laboratory-scale works. But for me, it's the same whether I do a painting which I would describe as a studio work, or a work of unlimited scale. I continue to experiment. I believe that art is a science, or a form of science.

C-LR You often say that art is the science of what cannot be proved by any other means.

JRS Precisely. This is my belief, and one which I expressed at the time of my exhibition at the Stedelijk Museum in Amsterdam: "The immaterial is the sensory reality of the universe. Art is the sensory knowledge of the immaterial. To become conscious of the immaterial in its state of pure structure, is to make the final leap towards the absolute."

I cannot conceive of art in any other sense, and as soon as you begin to think in this way, you come upon a fabulous world which has never been explored. That's why whenever I hear anyone say that abstract art is dead (a current view around 1950) I have to laugh.

C-LR You often say that you would have no sense of accomplishment if you were to remain at the point of discovering only phenomena; you have to communicate these phenomena to others, and their reactions are important to you.

JRS   If I continue to create works of art, it is mainly to demonstrate to others the phenomena that I've discovered. Personally, as I've already said, I could do without this, but I want to awaken people, to interest them in knowledge of universal phenomena, as foreseen by the artist, the scientist, the philosopher. . . .

C-LR   From your life, your work and from everything you say, there emerges an impression of deep and serious respect for artistic creation, at once as a means of knowing the world, and as a way of communicating with others. You don't enclose yourself within an egotistical isolation but are willing to pay the price of the social responsibilities you have assumed.

But, as opposed to a number of your contemporaries, it is through the work of art itself (even to the point of metamorphozing it completely, to make it compatible with the arrested framework of our life) that you have chosen to act. You have an optimistic belief in the work to be done, in its very permanence, while others want to move farther in the direction of the ephemeral, spontaneous intervention, and finally, towards the negation of the work itself.

JRS   Listen, in the beginning, I, too, was interested in the ephemeral work of art, because it then seemed to me a way of seizing the universal character of a given moment. But I abandoned this mode when I began to realize that even the ephemeral things I made were not really ephemeral. People always found a way, in one fashion or another, to reconstruct them, and even if they couldn't reconstruct them, the work remained rigidly fixed in their minds.

C-LR   Your attitude, moreover, is just as clear when it comes to the relationship between art and politics. You aren't one of those who directly relate your explorations in art to whatever political positions you espouse.

JRS   Yes, I separate art and politics because I view politics as a series of transitory phases; if I submitted my work to politics, my art would lose whatever solidity it has. I would have to deviate from my speculative method. I would gradually have to abandon my experiments as an artist to political demands. I find it altogether normal that a politician should give priority to politics, but for me, an artist, my own priority is the domain of art.

C-LR   For several years now, your activities have served as a response to those who spend their time debating the role of the artist in society; you spent a great deal of your time, energy and money to establish a Museum of Contemporary Art in Ciudad Bolivar, to which you donated most of the art, not only your own, but works by other artists as well. I find it really inspiring that a noted artist, especially one who has half of his creative life ahead of him, should devote his efforts to such a project, instead of finally enjoying his own hard-won independence.

JRS   I've never forgotten the difficulties which I experienced in trying to discover and understand art. In Ciudad Bolivar, I would like to help educate young people so that they wouldn't have to struggle against the same obstacles. If I can give them that, I would be very happy.

I took such pains with this project because I wanted to create, in some complete form, in the village where I had such a difficult beginning, something which would serve as a point of departure for those interested in art. If I succeed—if only two or three artists emerge in the future—I will be happy. I would feel I had won. And even if no artists come forth, the Museum will have helped inform the people of Ciudad Bolivar and the surrounding villages who are beginning to visit it. This is simply pedagogic desire on my part, born from the certainty that, in terms of universal phenomena, the reactions of a man from a so-called under-developed country and from an over-developed one, are the same.

Don't forget that despite great strides forward, I come from a country which, when I left it for the first time, was still considered very backward. I come from a country which has yet to build its own world. For us, the problem is not what to destroy. I can easily understand how a country like Germany would create Expressionist art, how the United States, which has achieved such a high standard of living, wants to go backwards, to return to its origins, how in France and Italy, they worry about re-examining the whole question of the pursuit of happiness. We don't have happiness as yet. First we must attain it, then we will see whether something must be destroyed in order to wake us up from it. But we haven't reached that point yet. First we must build, create happiness, conquer it. . . .

Extraits d'entretiens de Soto

avec Claude-Louis Renard
Paris, 1974

RENARD Soto, au moment d'exposer au Guggenheim Museum de New-York, si vous oubliez quelques instants l'artiste capital que vous êtes devenu, que vous le revendiquez ou non, et si vous vous retournez vers l'enfant et l'adolescent qui vivait au Vénézuela, dans son pays, à Ciudad-Bolivar, avant la dernière guerre mondiale, pouvez-vous situer votre première rencontre avec l'art?

SOTO Ma vraie première rencontre, je l'ai eue, si on peut parler d'art professionnel, en arrivant à Caracas en 1942, quand j'ai eu une toute petite bourse pour faire des études aux Beaux-Arts. Mais je peux vous assurer que je n'ai jamais fait d'autre métier à proprement parler. J'ai fait mes études à l'école primaire, puis j'ai commencé à travailler à Ciudad-Bolivar: ce n'était pas de l'art pur, c'était de l'art appliqué, je peignais des affiches pour le cinéma. Je me suis fait rapidement une petite réputation de peintre, qui m'a permis de demander cette bourse pour aller étudier à Caracas. Cependant la plupart de mes souvenirs d'enfance sont, en dehors de la ville, les paysages et les longues années que j'ai passées à la campagne.

C-LR Vous avez continué de dessiner après vos premiers essais. Etait-ce toujours un besoin spontané, un plaisir simple et direct, ou déjà une réaction à des oeuvres d'autres artistes, même découvertes par des reproductions ?

JRS Non. A Ciudad-Bolivar, il n'existait rien du tout ; je n'avais, par exemple, jamais vu un chevalet. La première fois que j'en ai vu un, c'était à l'Ecole des Beaux-Arts, à Caracas.

C-LR J'ai toujours été frappé par le long temps pendant lequel vous avez travaillé comme peintre, mais sans aucune référence culturelle. Vous vous êtes formé seul, au bout du monde, où personne ne vous aidait.

JRS Non, je ne dirais pas que personne ne m'a aidé, parce que tout de même mes vieux maîtres étaient des artistes, presque tous autodidactes, formés à travers les revues d'art et les quelques livres qui arrivaient difficilement à Caracas. Ils savaient très

22

bien qu'ils ne pouvaient pas aller plus loin que l'impressionnisme, ils ne comprenaient déjà pas très bien le cubisme, mais ils avaient le courage de nous montrer les quelques reproductions d'oeuvres du cubisme qu'ils avaient pu trouver d'une façon ou d'une autre, et généralement à travers des revues très quelconques. Mais je pense que ces hommes ont déclenché en moi l'esprit de recherche. Même s'ils n'en étaient pas capables eux-mêmes, ils ont toujours stimulé ma démarche vers l'inconnu dans l'art au lieu de m'imposer leur propre manière de peindre. Je leur en suis très reconnaissant et je suis très heureux de retrouver à Caracas ceux qui sont encore vivants, car beaucoup sont morts, c'étaient des hommes en général très âgés.

C-LR   A Caracas, quelle a été la première oeuvre qui vous a marqué réellement ?

JRS   La chose qui m'a le plus frappé en arrivant à Caracas, je l'ai souvent raconté, c'était une nature morte cubiste de Braque, elle était posée sur un chevalet ; et cette oeuvre m'a beaucoup étonné. Ce qui est curieux, c'est qu'en arrivant de Ciudad-Bolivar, au lieu de m'intéresser à un art descriptif ou autre, j'aie été précisément attiré par cette oeuvre-là.

   Je demandais à des artistes, à des étudiants déjà avancés dans leurs études, des précisions sur cette oeuvre, je cherchais avec eux pourquoi elle m'intéressait et pourquoi elle était en quelque sorte mise en vedette à l'entrée de l'école. Ils ont été très honnêtes, ils m'ont dit que je ne pouvais évidemment pas comprendre d'emblée, que c'était un art difficile, qu'il fallait étudier sérieusement pour approfondir son contenu. Alors, pour moi, il s'agissait d'étudier, d'investiguer, et, dès la fin de la première année, j'étais déjà au courant de ce qu'étaient le cubisme et les dernières démarches de Picasso.

C-LR   Vous manifestiez déjà à cet âge cette volonté acharnée de comprendre, de remonter aux sources, qui est enracinée au plus profond de vous et qui ne vous a jamais quitté, ainsi que cette attraction qui vous conduit infailliblement vers ce qui est neuf.

JRS   Oui, surtout que, venant de Ciudad-Bolivar, je n'avais pas de connaissances sur l'art en général. J'avais vu des reproductions de l'Angélus de Millet, et sûrement quelques chromos de madones de Murillo qui ne m'attiraient pas beaucoup. Quand je vous écoute parler, je suis moi aussi étonné de m'être intéressé à une oeuvre cubiste plutôt qu'à une oeuvre plus figurative. Je me suis mis d'ailleurs tout de suite à travailler à fond pour découvrir les racines de l'oeuvre de Braque, et à partir de celle-ci j'ai compris Picasso. Remontant un peu en arrière, les oeuvres de Cézanne et de van Gogh se sont révélées à moi. J'ai été vaguement attiré à un moment donné par Gauguin, je n'étais pas tout à fait convaincu par ses formes, sa façon de voir symbolique, mais j'aimais malgré tout sa couleur. Plus tard à Paris, lorsque je vis les oeuvres originales, je fus très déçu car cette même couleur m'apparut fade. Voilà mes premiers souvenirs de l'Ecole des Beaux-Arts.

C-LR   Y avait-il déjà à Caracas les bases d'une documentation, des reproductions, des revues?

JRS   Il y avait seulement quelques reproductions, une petite bibliothèque qui contenait des documents sur l'histoire de l'art jusqu'à l'impressionnisme. Après, beaucoup plus tard, sont arrivés quelques livres sur le cubisme, le fauvisme, mais c'était déjà la fin de mes études.

C-LR   Avez-vous eu l'occasion de voir, à cette époque, un ou plusieurs tableaux de ces artistes ?

JRS   La dernière année, je suis allé voir une collection privée où il y avait, parmi d'autres, des Sisley et des Dunoyer de Segonzac. Là, j'ai vu pour la première fois des tableaux de peintres. Mais je ne comprenais pas vraiment l'oeuvre impressionniste au Vénézuela, car la lumière impressionniste ne correspond pas à la lumière tropicale qui est très franche, très forte. J'ai été vraiment émerveillé quand je suis arrivé au petit matin, pour la première fois, aux environs de

Paris : j'ai vu les bouleaux un peu rougeâtres, c'était déjà le début de l'automne, et j'ai compris à ce moment là pourquoi les impressionnistes ont peint comme ils l'ont fait.

C-LR A Caracas, tout en terminant vos études, vous continuiez à dessiner, à peindre pour vous?

JRS Oui, et je suis retourné à Ciudad-Bolivar où je devais être professeur parce qu'on m'avait donné une bourse à cette condition mais on n'a pas voulu de moi. Par contre, on m'a appelé à Maracaibo pour diriger la petite Ecole des Beaux-Arts. L'élève le plus assidu là-bas, c'était moi ; je peignais, jour et nuit, tant que je pouvais. Je n'ai jamais pu convaincre mes élèves de suivre la même démarche, de travailler sérieusement, à l'exception d'une jeune dame qui a continué et qui, aujourd'hui, est l'âme de Maracaibo. Elle a gardé cette espèce de flamme et a converti la ville à l'art moderne.

C-LR A Maracaibo, qu'est-ce que vous peigniez à l'époque?

JRS Je cherchais en partant du cubisme, mais il est évident que, comme je n'avais aucun élément sur ce qui avait suivi, j'ai été arrêté par mon ignorance. Je savais que le cubisme s'était développé avant la première guerre, alors je me demandais ce qui s'était passé entre cette période et les années 1948-1950. Il avait dû se passer des choses formidables que j'ignorais. Je me disais que je ne devais pas chercher tout seul des choses qui étaient certainement déjà faites, déjà résolues . . .

C-LR . . . En évoquant vos débuts vous faites apparaître tout naturellement deux traits fondamentaux de votre caractère que j'ai eu souvent l'occasion de retrouver au cours des travaux d'intégration à l'architecture que vous avez poursuivis, en liaison avec mes activités, ces deux dernières années: d'abord, un manque d'intérêt total pour les chemins déjà tracés et, au contraire, une volonté acharnée de recherche vers des zones non encore défrichées.

24

Par ailleurs, une conscience, même informulée, de l'immense travail à fournir pour réaliser effectivement ces recherches, d'où une économie de moyens très sévère, une attention à ne pas se laisser aller au dilettantisme, un sens très aigu de ce qui est essentiel et de ce qui ne l'est pas pour assurer votre survie créatrice à vos propres yeux.

Dans le fond, cette évidence, pour vous, que quelque chose s'était passé en Europe qui vous échappait vous était intolérable, et j'imagine que cela a dû contribuer fortement à vous décider à partir pour Paris.

JRS C'est même la seule raison, il n'y en a aucune autre. Je suis venu là où je pensais trouver le matériel que je ne connaissais pas. Et très vite, je me suis mis au courant, j'ai commencé à faire mes petites études personnelles sur l'art abstrait.

C-LR A cette époque, avant de quitter le Vénézuela, comment vivait Soto ? Vous peigniez, vous dessiniez presque sans arrêt, mais étiez-vous déjà en même temps un homme pris par la musique, viviez-vous comme maintenant ou étiez-vous assez différent ?

JRS Non, c'était vraiment pareil et les amis qui m'ont connu à l'époque trouvent que je n'ai pas du tout changé de comportement vis-à-vis des gens et de moi-même.

Je continue à aimer la musique, à vivre de façon très détendue, à voir des amis; dès que je peux faire une fête, je la fais. Je ne mêle pas mes sentiments spontanés et mon besoin de construire un art tout à fait raisonné, ce sont deux choses que je n'ai jamais voulu mélanger. De nombreuses personnes ont cru trouver une influence de la musique sur mon travail; il est fort possible qu'elle y soit présente, mais alors pas dans le sens de la musique populaire que je pratique, plutôt dans le sens de la musique de Bach, à travers sa structure dégagée. Mais je ne vois pas pourquoi un homme qui fait des démarches très serrées dans une direction ne pourrait pas, par ailleurs, s'épanouir comme tout le monde.

-LR Il me semble qu'au-delà de l'homme Soto que l'on voit se laisser vivre, se détendre pendant une fête, jouer de la guitare, parler avec ses amis, se promener, aller au café, il y a l'homme plus secret, non pas caché au sens étroit du mot, mais qui se protège, se met à l'abri : deux heures de sommeil, prendre vite l'avion pour changer de pays, s'isoler dans un coin et laisser les gens parler entre eux, s'abstraire même d'un contexte qu'il aime pour revenir inéxorablement à son travail. Est-ce ainsi que vous vous voyez ?

JRS Oui, dans n'importe quelle circonstance, même s'il y a une fête, s'il se présente quelqu'un de vraiment intéressé ou intéressant dans le domaine de l'art tel que je le conçois, j'oublie tout et je laisse tout tomber pour m'y consacrer, car, au fond, c'est cela qui compte le plus pour moi. Je ne dis pas que le reste ne m'intéresse pas, mais la possibilité de développer cette démarche dans laquelle je me suis engagé est ce qui me nourrit constamment. Si mon destin était celui d'un scientifique, je ferais sans doute la même chose, je poursuivrais mon investigation sur un plan essentiellement spéculatif.

C-LR Cette obstination vous a certainement aidé pour acquérir cette culture très originale, étendue, et pas du tout livresque ni théorique, très aiguë, qui passe tout au crible sans complaisance. On a l'impression que, sans arrêt, chez vous, derrière votre approche sensible, l'esprit critique est en alerte. Pour chaque artiste, vous allez à l'essentiel et vous vous posez la question: qu'est-ce qu'il a apporté ? Est-ce qu'il a fait avancer, même si peu que ce soit, l'histoire de l'art, ou bien a t-il seulement répété ? Est-ce un suiveur ou a t-il fait progresser quelque chose ?

JRS Oui, parce qu'il n'y a pas de création autrement. Sinon, on fait de l'art naïf. Si on n'est pas vraiment un professionnel, si on ne conçoit pas l'art comme un apport à la culture, alors il faut rester à Ciudad-Bolivar et faire de l'art naïf comme tout le monde, comme quantité d'artistes dans le monde. L'art naïf est une façon de s'exprimer, sans doute, mais, au fond, cela n'ajoute rien, ça reste toujours identique partout, c'est plutôt un témoignage de la sensibilité humaine, ce n'est pas un témoignage de l'évolution culturelle.

C-LR Comment définiriez-vous dans ce domaine ce qui
vous apparaît nouveau par rapport à ce qui n'est
que répétition ?

JRS C'est très simple : l'histoire de l'art, la vraie, celle
qui me tient à coeur, qui m'intéresse, évidemment
ce n'est pas moi qui l'invente au départ, elle a été
définie par une quantité de créateurs, de penseurs,
c'est comme un mur qui grandit par la superposition
et l'adjonction des apports successifs. D'autres
possibilités se présentent sans cesse parallèlement,
à côté, ce sont peut-être des stimulants pour les
créateurs, mais la plus importante, c'est celle qui
continue à évoluer tout droit. C'est une idée très
positiviste, si vous voulez, mais je pense que l'art
doit être positiviste. Il doit contribuer à la formation
de la société, à un niveau très professionnel ;
puisque nous sommes des artistes formés dans le
monde occidental, avec la pensée occidentale, l'art
doit évoluer avec le même sérieux, du même pas
que la philosophie, l'investigation scientifique, les
mathématiques, etc . . . Pour moi l'art est valable à
partir du moment où cette évolution est justifiée
rationnellement . . .

C-LR . . . Vous quittez le Vénézuela, vous arrivez à Paris
en 1950, qu'est-ce que vous y trouvez d'abord ? Bien
sûr des Sud-Américains, des amis, car je ne vous
vois pas restant tout seul.

JRS Non, au contraire. Une bande d'amis était partie un
peu avant moi, une année auparavant, je leur ai
écrit, ils m'ont attendu et ont été vraiment très
gentils avec moi. Toute l'information qu'ils avaient,
je l'ai pompée tout de suite. J'ai pris tous leurs livres
et, avec un dictionnaire, je me suis mis à travailler
jusqu'à cinq heures du matin pour traduire car je ne
connaissais pas un mot de français. Trois mois
après, j'avais pratiquement lu tous ces livres et
j'avais toutes les informations possibles. C'est ainsi
qu'ils m'ont mis en contact avec le salon annuel des
Réalités Nouvelles et tous les artistes qu'ils con-
naissaient à l'époque. J'ai connu comme ça autour
de Denise René tous les artistes qui, à ce moment

là, étaient à mes yeux des chercheurs. J'ai eu l'occasion de beaucoup parler avec eux. Puis je suis parti voir les oeuvres de Mondrian et de Malévich.

C-LR Où les avez-vous vues ?

JRS Je pensais les trouver à Paris, mais, comme il n'y en avait pas, j'ai dû aller un peu vers le Nord, en Hollande.

C-LR Au Stedelijk Museum d'Amsterdam et au Kröller-Müller à Otterloo ?

JRS Oui, exactement.

C-LR Il ne devait pas exister par ailleurs beaucoup de livres sur eux.

JRS Non, il y avait seulement quelques articles, puis le premier livre sur Moholy-Nagy est arrivé vers l'année 1954 en anglais. Je l'ai acheté et j'ai trouvé quelqu'un de bénévole, une dame très intellectuelle qui, gentiment, m'a traduit deux ou trois pages par nuit jusqu'à ce que j'aie lu tout le livre.

C-LR J'admire une fois de plus la façon dont vous êtes construit tout seul vous-même, pas à pas, comme un artisan qui vérifie chaque fois la qualité de ses matériaux et de ses outils, et cela sans en avoir l'air, en laissant les autres croire que votre vie est facile, que vous vous laissez vivre, alors que cette non-chalance superficielle cache une immense volonté absolument infatigable de trouver coûte que coûte les éléments de tous ordres indispensables à la poursuite de votre constitution.

JRS Je le fais en pleine conscience, j'ai toujours voulu que ce que je possède soit sûr. Si je me trompe, tant pis ; ce n'est pas que je cherche à me tromper, mais ce que j'ai toujours voulu c'est que le peu que je possède je le sente très solide pour pouvoir continuer. Je sais qu'aujourd'hui j'ai une expérience qui m'appartient, que je la possède très solidement, et ça me permet de continuer à travailler. Même si

un certain succès ne m'était pas venu, j'aurais persisté de la même façon. Je crois que je n'aurais jamais fléchi.

C-LR Dans le fond, vous n'avez été réellement connu, au-delà des amis, qu'autour de 1960, après la Biennale de Venise, bien que vous ayez participé en 1955 à l'Exposition Le Mouvement chez Denise René qui groupait pour la première fois les principaux artistes travaillant alors dans des directions voisines de la vôtre. Auparavant, c'était le travail souterrain, le tunnel. Mais vous êtes resté à Paris, alors que vous auriez très bien pu ne pas y rester, aller vous fixer ailleurs.
Vous vous sentiez bien à Paris ?

JRS Oui, très bien.

C-LR Vers quoi votre intérêt se portait-il essentiellement alors ?

JRS D'abord une des choses qui m'a marqué, c'est une histoire sur Malévich d'une fille à Maracaïbo qui avait une façon méprisante de me parler de Blanc sur Blanc du Museum of Modern Art de New-York, alors que pour moi c'est devenu une espèce de guide spirituel. Et puis, en arrivant ici, j'ai vu les reproductions de quelques oeuvres de Kandinsky qui commençaient à être publiées. Moi, je n'aime pas du tout le Kandinsky expressionniste, mais j'aime beaucoup le Kandinsky "Bauhaus", très construit. J'ai pris aussi contact avec l'oeuvre de Sophie Taeuber, j'ai connu Arp, et avec cet acquis j'ai discuté énormément avec d'autres artistes et particulièrement avec mes amis latino-américains dont le nombre et l'importance sont considérables. J'étais plutôt attiré par les oeuvres qui sont sorties de l'esprit "Bauhaus" et, dans Klee, par les oeuvres qui recherchent la perspective à plusieurs points de vue. Cela m'a beaucoup intéressé. Il est évident que je laisse de côté tout le symbolisme de Klee, mais quand il devient profond à mes yeux, c'est une cathédrale. J'ai découvert, avec beaucoup de difficultés, l'oeuvre d'Albers parce qu'il n'y avait presque rien ici. Je me suis informé tant que j'ai pu, et finalement Denise René a décidé de faire venir quelques oeuvres et a fait une exposition. Voilà ce dont je me rappelle : Mondrian, Malévich, Klee, Albers, et les amis avec qui je discutais . . .

C-LR . . . Comment se développaient vos propres travaux depuis votre arrivée à Paris ?

JRS D'abord, dans une première période, j'ai voulu dynamiser les oeuvres de Mondrian que j'aimais beaucoup, car je trouvais que l'issue était de les faire bouger. Je ne sais pas, c'est une question d'intuition. Jusqu'au moment où j'ai connu les *Broadway Boogie-Woogie* et où j'ai compris que Mondrian avait déjà résolu ce problème.

C-LR Vous réagissez de nouveau comme vous l'aviez fait vis-à-vis des cubistes : la recherche est déjà faite, les solutions trouvées, ce n'est pas la peine de perdre son temps à répéter.

JRS Oui, puisque cela est fini, il faut continuer plus loin. Comme ça, j'ai commencé à gratter un peu partout, j'ai trouvé la démarche de Moholy-Nagy très importante, incomplète sans doute à cause de sa mort prématurée, mais il était l'un des artistes les plus doués de cette époque. J'ai découvert aussi Calder, Marcel Duchamp et Gabo. A partir de ces créateurs j'ai commencé à construire un monde en me disant qu'il fallait que je reprenne tous les éléments qu'ils avaient dégagés, mais qu'ils n'avaient pas fait aboutir, que je devais essayer de trouver des réponses à toutes les questions qu'ils avaient posées, mais pas solutionnées, à ce que nous appelons en espagnol des *planteamientos.*

C-LR Des questions restées en suspens ? C'est toujours l'homme de recherche qui réapparaît.

JRS Oui, j'ai commencé à travailler pour résoudre ces problèmes non résolus par les autres artistes, et je suis finalement tombé dans mon véritable travail. J'ai compris qu'il y avait quelque chose qui m'appartenait, j'ai commencé à développer ma propre démarche, tout en gardant le respect pour les artistes qui m'avaient guidé.

C-LR Et est-ce que vous êtes d'accord pour dire que les premières oeuvres qui ont concrétisé cette recherche sont les *Répétitions* de 1951 ?

JRS Oui. La répétition possède un caractère universel, elle révèle des structures pures, c'est une idée de base.

C-LR Il s'agit déjà d'une désindividualisation, de cette désindividualisation qu'on retrouve à la racine de tous vos travaux.

JRS Pour faire un art vraiment abstrait — quand je dis abstrait j'emploie ce mot dans toute sa signification — il faut se dépersonnaliser, il faut que la situation de chaque individu ne compte plus. Pour m'épanouir et canaliser ma vie personnelle, je préfère réunir mes amis, organiser avec eux des fêtes, mais je ne veux pas donner à mon travail un contenu directement individuel.

C-LR Il semble que toute la richesse de votre vie personnelle n'est là que pour permettre à votre travail de voir le jour dans des conditions favorables. Et finalement c'est le travail qui, malgré les apparences, ordonne le tout.

JRS Oui, même les vacances, pour moi ce sont des vacances de travail. Je n'arrive pas à m'épanouir comme tout le monde à la plage, ce n'est pas possible. Une heure couché à la plage à simplement oublier le monde, c'est un moment perdu. J'adore le soleil, mais il faut que je continue à réfléchir sur ma démarche.

C-LR Combien de fois m'avez-vous dit pendant la préparation du projet d'intégration pour les nouveaux bâtiments de Renault : "Redites-moi le problème à résoudre, pendant le voyage j'y penserai". Vous reveniez et, tout en ayant fait des quantités de choses, la solution était là. Vous aviez continué d'y travailler sans réelle interruption. . . .
    La répétition, c'est la première dépersonnalisation, c'est la première désindividualisation, "désanimisation" comme vous le dites, mais ensuite vous utilisez la progression qui accentue cette voie.

JRS La répétition est une valeur abstraite, inscrite parfaitement dans l'universel.
    La progression est une variante de la répétition, avec une donnée non absolue : le point de départ. Pour l'universaliser, il faut concevoir la progression cyclique où le point de départ perd sa valeur particulière.
    Et puis j'ai lu, tout seul, des livres sur la musique sérielle. J'avais toujours eu une grande admiration pour l'organisation d'un monde fabuleux à partir d'éléments très simples et abstraits, comme dans l'oeuvre de Bach. De même, découvrir qu'avec la même série on pouvait construire un monde nouveau m'a beaucoup impressionné : moi aussi, vers 1953, pour résoudre mon problème, j'ai tenté de codifier les couleurs de base afin d'établir un système sériel. On me demande pourquoi je n'ai pas continué à faire des oeuvres "sérielles", c'est tout simplement parce que l'oeuvre sérielle m'a rapidement amené vers une étape nouvelle, celle des oeuvres vibratoires qui sont devenues le but de mes recherches.

C-LR Oui, une période était terminée, vous aviez trouvé ce que vous cherchiez en partant des *Répétitions*, et en arrivant aux *Progressions* et aux oeuvres sérielles. . . .
    Je crois comme vous qu'il ne s'agit pas ici de procéder à une analyse théorique de votre démarche, mais d'essayer de donner au public des précisions lui permettant de mieux situer vos oeuvres à la fois dans le contexte de votre vie et par rapport aux travaux de vos contemporains ou de ceux dont vous revendiquez l'importance. Toutefois, pourriez-vous dégager à partir des premières oeuvres vibratoires, les principales étapes de votre développement ?

JRS Les oeuvres sérielles issues des *Répétitions* avaient donné naissance à la vibration optique du tableau. Je suis passé presque immédiatement à la superposition de deux vibrations, de deux répétitions, et aux progressions superposées. Et c'est à partir de cette superposition que je suis arrivé au mouvement optique par le déplacement du spectateur devant l'oeuvre fixe. D'abord ce sont les tableaux comme *Métamorphoses,* exposé aux Réalités Nouvelles en 1954, avec une grille décalée où, déjà, la question du temps intervient. Ensuite, j'ai fait *La Petite boîte de Villanueva,* avec ses trois plaques transparentes, striées sur toute leur surface à l'exception d'un carré sans strie sur chaque plaque : cela créait une espèce d'espace ambigu et des mouvements optiques. De là, je suis passé à la *Spirale* et á mes autres oeuvres en plexiglas. J'avais beaucoup travaillé pour me rendre compte de la présence du temps dans l'art et pour arriver à la rendre perceptible : j'avais découvert un élément que je devais développer. J'ai fait à ce moment là je ne sais combien d'oeuvres en plexiglas, dont beaucoup ont disparu. Petit à petit, en mettant des éléments suspendus librement entre le plexiglas et le fond opaque, tous deux striés, je me suis aperçu que leurs mouvements pouvaient s'intégrer aux vibrations optiques, et je suis parvenu aux objets suspendus que vous connaissez: "courbes immatérielles," tiges, etc. . . . qui, par le jeu des déplacements, disparaissent pour ne former plus que des vibrations.

C-LR A partir des plexiglas, il était devenu évident que l'oeuvre d'art telle que vous la conceviez, si elle était toujours, bien entendu, au départ, votre création, ne pouvait exister sans la participation active du spectateur qui, par son mouvement, faisait apparaître les vibrations que vous y aviez introduites. Et vous n'avez cessé de demander au spectateur de jouer ce rôle dans toutes les oeuvres qui ont suivi. Cette participation du spectateur étant, comme la désindividualisation et l'universalisation, inséparable désormais de votre travail.

JRS J'ai continué ainsi pendant près de deux ans, j'ai découvert l'infinité de possibilités que m'offrait la superposition de deux surfaces tramées. J'avais conscience d'être en train de chercher des valeurs pour construire quelque chose plus tard, mais je voyais que ce n'étaient pas des éléments encore tout à fait contrôlés par moi, ils restaient presque trop complètement libres.

C-LR Vous apprivoisiez quelque chose de nouveau.

JRS Voilà. A un moment donné, j'ai compris qu'il me fallait éliminer une des deux libertés, et c'est comme cela que, à partir de 1957, j'ai gardé simplement la trame du fond très serrée, presque mécanique, et laissé la liberté à la partie superposée. J'en suis venu à le démarche presque baroque que vous connaissez, avec du matériel hétéroclite pour me prouver que tous les éléments étaient valables pour cela. Quand j'ai compris que tout était possible, je me suis de nouveau mis à contrôler ces éléments et j'ai choisi ceux qui étaient les plus simples, les plus adaptés à ma démarche.

C-LR Pour traduire cette universalité, vous faites appel aux moyens matériels les plus simples avec un souci d'économie et d'efficacité qui ne vous quitte jamais.

JRS Vous savez, je viens d'un pays, le Vénézuela, où, lorsque j'étais jeune, tout restait à faire, et pour le faire, on ne pouvait compter que sur ses propres moyens. Je vous l'ai dit, j'ai cherché jusqu'au moment où j'ai pu trouver exactement ce que je voulais, et j'ai acquis peu à peu par mon travail un langage me permettant de montrer mes découvertes.

C-LR Dans toutes les rétrospectives que j'ai vues de vos oeuvres en Europe, j'ai toujours été saisi par l'évidence d'une réussite tout à fait merveilleuse, d'autant plus merveilleuse qu'elle s'est répété à plusieurs reprises de façon nouvelle à travers des séries différentes : cette réussite qui consiste à parvenir, pour chaque problème posé, à la solution la plus directe, la plus pure, en rendant les éléments les plus simples capables de transmettre exactement les phénomènes que vous aviez isolés et que vous vouliez faire percevoir.

JRS Je veux travailler jusqu'à ce que j'y parvienne, je tiens à cette économie de moyens.

C-LR Pour moi, les oeuvres qui se sont succédées de 1962 à 1967, les *Courbes immatérielles,* avec leurs tiges de métal horizontales et identiques, suspendues par des fils de nylon devant une surface uniformément tramée, les *Carrés vibratoires,* les *Tiges suspendues parallèles,* et plus récemment, les *T,* cristallisent sur votre parcours les jalons de vos découvertes, et ont atteint une perfection définitive. Et nous retrouverons plus loin cette même qualité, cette même netteté dans le propos, avec vos oeuvres s'inscrivant dans un espace plus vaste, qu'il s'agisse des *Pénétrables* ou des *Extensions* et des *Progressions au sol* à partir de 1968.

En ce qui me concerne, je mets un peu à part des oeuvres auxquelles, vous le savez, je suis particulièrement attaché, celles que vous appelez *Ecritures.* D'une certaine façon on peut y trouver, je crois, comme un retour singulier à la trace directe de la main de l'artiste, peut-être aussi, tout en restant cohérent avec votre volonté de désindividualisation, une transcription plus immédiate de votre sensibilité personnelle, comme une permission accordée plus ou moins consciemment à votre main d'agir plus librement. Il s'agit là d'un domaine assez secret, chaque fois redécouvert, comme si on assistait à quelque chose d'indiscret par rapport au reste de votre oeuvre.

JRS C'est possible. Les *Ecritures* sont pour moi une façon de dessiner dans l'espace.

Cruz-Diez, avec qui j'ai fait mes études, m'a dit devant les premières *Ecritures* : "C'est ton langage, ce sont les mêmes signes, comme lorsque tu as voulu dépasser Mondrian." C'est vrai, je n'y avais même pas songé. C'était aussi avec des courbes comme ça qu'étaient dessinés mes paysages. Il est fort possible que, si j'avais été un peintre du XVIIIe siècle, ma main aurait dessiné d'instinct avec des traits analogues. Peut-être . . . Mais même dans cette liberté, je continue, vous voyez, à conserver une structure, à contrôler tout de même les éléments . . .

C-LR Il semble que le décalage entre la trame impersonnelle du fond et les tiges pliées ou courbées au gré de votre liberté, vous a permis de créer là un langage capable de contenir le maximum d'individualité compatible avec votre volonté d'universalité. Même dans ces *Ecritures,* les vibrations pures sont loin d'être absentes, naissant des tiges verticales qui ponctuent le rythme des courbes et des lignes brisées.

De toutes façons, ces incursions furtives d'une main qui ne traduit pas d'ailleurs votre "statement" sont rares et ne vous ont jamais entraîné en dehors de votre territoire.

JRS Non. J'ai toujours continué à travailler dans la même direction, et ces *Ecritures* se sont intercalées de façon intermittente entre des recherches plus rigoureuses et contrôlées . . .

C-LR Comment réagissiez-vous aux travaux des artistes qui avaient pris des directions complètement différentes des vôtres, suiviez-vous leur travail ?

C'est certainement l'un des traits caractéristiques de notre temps que des démarches en apparence radicalement opposées, se situant sur des orbites très éloignées, puissent coexister et poursuivre chacune leur destinée sans interférence. Ainsi, à mesure que vous atteignez une dépersonnalisation et une universalité par la mise en évidence de la matière originelle, d'autres artistes refusent au contraire toute perte de leur individualité. Dubuffet par exemple s'acharne à capter le grouillement de la vie constituée, de l'organique plus ou moins indifférencié aux surgissements les plus abrupts de l'imaginaire.

JRS Oui, c'est un tout autre chemin, mais je le respecte. . . .

C-LR . . . Si l'on revient à votre oeuvre en 1968, vous avez donc délimité, à la suite d'expériences successives, le champ de vos recherches. Vous avez fait aboutir jusqu'à leur expression la plus évidente les préoccupations qui vous ont tenu en haleine pendant plus de quinze ans, et vous êtes l'auteur d'une oeuvre cohérente qui a déjà pris une place capitale dans l'évolution de l'art contemporain. Il me semble pourtant que les années 1968 et 1969 constituent à nouveau pour vous une charnière importante pour trois ordres de facteurs : en effet, d'abord vous disposez de moyens matériels sans commune mesure avec ceux de vos débuts, qui vous permettent de vous libérer et de réaliser des oeuvres à une échelle beaucoup plus vaste comme le *Cube à espace ambigu* ou les longs alignements droits ou courbes de tiges verticales aux dimensions mêmes de la salle où elles prennent place. La relation de l'oeuvre avec le spectateur s'accentue et change alors même de nature : celui-ci participait à l'oeuvre qui était en face de lui, maintenant ce spectateur et l'espace que vous avez investi deviennent indissociables. Cet apport révolutionnaire deviendra éclatant avec votre création des *Pénétrables* où le spectateur s'insère parmi les fils ou les tiges verticales qui ont envahi tout le volume disponible et constituent l'oeuvre, les anime, l'oeuvre et le spectateur, désormais physiquement mêlés inextricablement. Avec ces *Pénétrables,* vous aboutissez à matérialiser totalement votre sentiment profond de la situation de l'homme plongé dans un univers "plein" où matière, espace et temps ne font qu'un dans un continuum de vibrations infinies. Enfin, et c'est sans doute l'aspect le plus actuel de votre démarche, vous accordez désormais une place prépondérante à vos travaux d'intégration à l'architecture, qui sortent votre oeuvre du milieu spécialisé et la mêlent directement à la vie quotidienne de vos contemporains. Cette volonté de mettre à la portée des autres vos découvertes vous entraîne à accepter les contraintes inhérentes à toutes ces intégrations réalisées aujourd'hui, c'est-à-dire dans un cadre conçu par des hommes qui sont le plus souvent très en retard par rapport à des recherches comme les vôtres.

JRS Je les accepte. Ce n'est pas du temps perdu. C'est un travail qui me tient à coeur. Je ne vois pas pourquoi je refuserais de m'adapter à une situation qui est ce qu'elle est. Je commence à travailler malheureusement lorsque les projets sont déjà avancés puisque notre société en est encore à cette conception de notre travail. C'est un effort supplémentaire. J'attends tranquillement les maquettes et je fais ce qu'il faut pour intervenir avec le moins possible de concessions. Je crois que les gens qui passeront tous les jours dans le nouveau hall d'entrée des Usines Renault, par example, entre les piliers tramés, les blocs de carrés vibratoires et la grande *Ecriture* de trente mètres de long que réunira le plafond formé de 250.000 tiges suspendues au-dessus d'eux, découvriront quelque chose qui était en eux, mais dont ils n'avaient pas encore pris connaissance. . . .

Les *Pénétrables,* les nouvelles oeuvres au sol, les intégrations à l'architecture sont au fond l'aboutissement de toutes mes recherches antérieures. J'ai toujours travaillé en chercheur qui veut trouver quelque chose : comme l'oeuvre sérielle m'avait conduit à la vibration optique du tableau et les superpositions aux oeuvres vraiment en mouvement, la recherche d'un langage universel, de phrases types, d'éléments démonstratifs, m'a naturellement amené vers l'abstraction pure. Avec mon idée d'universel, il n'y a plus de mesure, je pourrais faire une oeuvre qui aille de Paris au Havre, qui traverse l'Océan, ce serait la même démarche. Simplement, pendant longtemps je n'ai pu faire que de petites oeuvres de laboratoire. Mais pour moi c'est identique, la réalisation d'un tableau que j'appelle plutôt une oeuvre d'atelier, et la création d'une oeuvre à échelle illimitée. Je continue à chercher. Je pense que l'art est une science, une forme de science.

C-LR Vous dites souvent que l'art est la science de ce qui ne peut pas être prouvé autrement.

JRS Exactement. Voilà mon opinion, je l'avais déjà exprimée au moment de mon exposition au Stedelijk Museum à Amsterdam : "L'Immatériel est la réalité sensible de l'univers. L'art est la connaissance sensible de l'immatériel. Prendre conscience de l'immatériel à l'état de structure pure, c'est franchir la dernière étape vers l'absolu."

Je ne conçois pas l'art autrement, et quand on pense comme cela on tombe sur un monde fabuleux qui n'a jamais été exploré. C'est pourquoi lorsque j'entends les gens dire que l'art abstrait est mort (ils le disaient déjà vers 1950) cela me fait rire.

C-LR   Vous dites aussi souvent que vous ne vous sentiriez pas quitte si vous découvriez seulement des phénomènes et que vous en restiez là. Vous avez un besoin de le communiquer aux autres, leurs réactions vous importent.

JRS   Si je continue à faire des oeuvres d'art, c'est bien pour démontrer aux autres des phénomènes que j'ai déjà découverts. Personnellement j'ai déjà dit que je pouvais me passer d'en faire, mais je veux éveiller les gens, les intéresser à la connaissance de phénomènes universels pressentis par l'artiste, le savant, le philosophe . . .

C-LR   . . . Il se dégage de votre vie, de votre travail, comme de tout ce que vous dites, un respect grave et sérieux pour la création artistique, à la fois comme moyen de connaissance du monde et comme moyen de communication avec les autres. Vous ne vous enfermez pas dans un isolement égoïste, vous payez le prix des responsabilités sociales que vous assumez.
   Mais contrairement à un certain nombre de vos contemporains, c'est à travers l'oeuvre d'art elle-même, quitte à la métamorphoser complètement et à la rendre compatible avec le cadre retardataire de notre vie, que vous avez choisi d'agir. Il y a chez vous une croyance optimiste dans l'oeuvre à construire, dans sa permanence même, alors que d'autres veulent tendre vers l'éphémère, l'intervention spontanée et finalement vers une négation de l'oeuvre elle-même.

JRS   Ecoutez, au début, j'ai été intéressé aussi par l'oeuvre éphémère parce que cela me paraissait un moyen de saisir le caractère universel d'un moment. Mais j'ai abandonné lorsque j'ai compris que même les choses éphémères que je construisais n'étaient jamais vraiment éphémères. Les gens trouvaient toujours le moyen, d'une façon ou d'une autre, de les reconstruire, et même s'ils ne pouvaient pas les reconstruire, dans leur tête ça restait figé.

-LR Votre attitude est d'ailleurs aussi nette en ce qui concerne les rapports de l'art et de la politique. Vous n'êtes pas de ceux qui mêlez directement vos recherches aux positions que vous pouvez avoir sur ce plan.

RS Oui, je sépare l'art et la politique parce que je considère que la politique est une suite d'étapes transitoires, et que si j'y soumets mon travail, il perdra la solidité que je lui ai donnée, je ferai dévier ma démarche spéculative, j'abandonnerai peu à peu ma recherche en tant qu'artiste au profit des besoins politiques. Dans la société, l'art est aussi important que la politique. Je trouve normal qu'un homme politique donne priorité à la politique, mais moi, en tant qu'artiste, je pense que je dois donner priorité à l'art.

LR Depuis plusieurs années vous avez répondu par des actes à ceux qui passent leur temps à débattre du rôle social de l'artiste, en consacrant beaucoup de votre temps, de vos forces et de votre argent, à créer le Musée d'Art Contemporain de Ciudad-Bolivar, pour lequel vous avez fourni l'essentiel des oeuvres, non pas seulement les vôtres, mais aussi celles des autres artistes. Je trouve poignant qu'un artiste célèbre, mais qui a encore la moitié de sa vie active devant lui, consacre tant d'effort à une telle oeuvre au lieu de profiter enfin d'une liberté si durement acquise.

RS Je n'ai jamais oubliées difficultés que j'ai eues pour découvrir et comprendre l'art. Je voudrais, à Ciudad-Bolivar, informer les jeunes pour éviter les mêmes difficultés. Si je peux leur offrir cela, je serai déjà très heureux.

La raison pour laquelle j'ai fait ce grand effort, c'est pour créer de toutes pièces, dans le village où j'avais eu tant de mal à mes débuts, quelque chose qui puisse servir de point de départ à ceux que cela intéresse. Si j'y réussis, même seulement pour deux ou trois artistes qui en sortiront dans l'avenir, je serai très content, j'aurai gagné. Et s'il n'y a pas d'artistes, ce Musée aura servi à informer les gens de Ciudad-Bolivar et des villages aux alentours qui commencent à venir le voir. C'est tout simplement

une volonté pédagogique, et la certitude que, vis-à-vis des phénomènes universels, les réactions d'un homme d'un pays soi-disant sous-développé et d'un pays soit-disant hyper-développé sont identiques.

N'oubliez pas, même si maintenant ça a beaucoup évolué, que je viens d'un pays qui, lorsque je l'ai quitté pour la première fois, était considéré plutôt comme très peu développé. Je suis d'un pays qui n'a pas encore construit son monde. Pour nous, il ne s'agit pas de détruire. Je comprends très bien qu'un pays comme l'Allemagne crée l'art expressionniste, que les Etats-Unis, qui ont atteint un haut standard de vie, veuillent faire marche arrière et revenir aux sources, qu'en France ou Italie, on se demande s'il faut remettre en question la recherche du bonheur. Nous, nous n'avons pas encore eu ce bonheur, nous devons d'abord l'atteindre. Après, on pourra essayer de voir si nous avons peut-être besoin de déchirer quelque chose pour nous réveiller de ce bonheur. En attendant, nous n'en sommes pas là, il faut d'abord construire, créer ce bonheur, le conquérir . . .

Extractos de entrevistas de Soto

con Claude-Louis Renard
Paris 1974

RENARD   Soto, en el momento en que Ud. expone en el Museo Guggenheim de Nueva York, si por un instante olvida al notable artista que es Ud. hoy, bien sea que lo pretenda o no, y se vuelve hacia el niño y el adolescente que vivía en Venezuela, en su país, en Ciudad Bolívar, antes de la última guerra mundial, ¿puede Ud. situar su primer encuentro con el arte?

SOTO   Mi primer encuentro verdadero lo tuve, si se puede hablar de arte profesional, al llegar a Caracas en 1942, cuando logré una pequeña beca para estudiar Bellas Artes. Pero yo le puedo asegurar que nunca hice otro oficio, propiamente hablando. Yo realicé mis estudios primarios, y luego empezé a trabajar en Ciudad Bolívar: no era arte puro, eran artes aplicadas, pues pintaba afiches para el cine. Rápidamente me creé una pequeña reputación de pintor, lo que me permitió solicitar aquella beca para ir a estudiar a Caracas. Sin embargo, la mayoría de mis recuerdos de infancia son, además de la ciudad, los paisajes y los largos años que pasé en el campo.

C-LR   Ud. siguió dibujando después de sus primeros ensayos. ¿Se trataba siempre de una necesidad espontánea, un placer simple y directo, o yá era una reacción suscitada por la obra de otros artistas, aún cuando la hubiera descubierto a través de reproducciones?

JRS   No. En Ciudad Bolívar, no existía nada; por ejemplo, yo nunca había visto un caballete. La primera vez que ví uno, fué en la Escuela de Bellas Artes, en Caracas.

C-LR   Siempre me ha impresionado el hecho de que durante largo tiempo haya Ud. trabajado como pintor, pero sin ninguna referencia cultural. Ud. se formó solo, allá en el fin del mundo, donde nadie lo ayudaba.

JRS   No, yo no diría que nadie me ha ayudado, porque de todas maneras mis viejos maestros eran artistas, casi todos autodidactas, formados a través de las revistas de arte y los pocos libros que llegaban con dificultad a Caracas. Ellos sabían muy bien que no podían ir más allá del impresionismo, e inclusive no podían comprender muy bien al cubismo; pero ellos tenían el valor de enseñarnos las reproducciones de obras del cubismo que habían podido encontrar de una manera u otra, generalmente mediante revistas muy corrientes. Pero yo pienso que estos hombres han desencadenado en mí el espíritu de búsqueda. Inclusive si ellos no eran capaces de buscar por sí mismos, estimularon siempre mi marcha hacia lo desconocido en el arte, en vez de imponerme su propia manera de pintar. Yo lo agradezco much y estoy muy contento de encontrar de nuevo en Caracas a aquellos que viven todavía, pues muchos de ellos han muerto; en general eran hombres de edad muy avanzada.

C-LR   En Caracas, ¿ cuál fue la primera obra que lo impresionó a Ud. realmente?

JRS   La cosa que más me impresionó cuando llegué a Caracas, y esto lo he contado frecuentemente, fue una naturaleza muerta cubista de Braque. Estaba colocada sobre un caballete, y me sorprendió mucho. Lo curioso es que llegando de Ciudad Bolívar, en lugar de interesarme por un arte descriptivo u otro, me haya sentido precisamente atraído por esa obra.

Yo preguntaba a los artistas, a alumnos yá bien adelantados en sus estudios, que me dieran precisiones sobre esa obra; buscaba con ellos por qué me interesaba y por qué estaba en cierto modo como puesta en un lugar destacado a la entrada de la Escuela. Ellos fueron muy honestos, me dijeron que evidentemente yo no podía comprender de golpe, que era un arte difícil y que era necesario estudiar seriamente para profundizar, en su contenido. Entonces, para mí, se trataba de estudiar, de investigar, y desde el fin del primer año yo estaba ya al corriente de lo que era el cubismo y las últimas producciones de Picasso.

C-LR   Entonces, yá a esa edad, Ud. manifestaba esa decidida voluntad de comprender, de llegar hasta las fuentes, que está arraigada en lo más profundo

de Ud. y que nunca le ha abandonado, lo mismo que esa atracción que le conduce infaliblemente hacia lo nuevo.

JRS   Sí. Sobre todo, viniendo de Ciudad Bolívar, yo carecía de conocimientos generales sobre el Arte. Había visto reproducciones del Angélus de Millet y seguramente algunos cromos de Vírgenes de Murillo que no me atraían mucho. Cuando le oigo hablar, también a mí me extraña el hecho de haberme interesado por una obra cubista más bien que por otra de carácter figurativo. En todo caso, me puse enseguida a trabajar seriamente para descubrir las raíces de la obra de Braque, y a partir de esta, comprendí a Picasso. Yendo luego un poco más atrás, también las obras de Cézanne y de van Gogh se revelaron a mí. En un momento me sentí vagamente atraído por Gauguin; yo no estaba del todo convencido por sus formas, por su manera de ver simbólica, pero a pesar de todo me gustaba su colorido. Más tarde, en París, cuando ví las obras originales, me sentí muy decepcionado porque ese mismo colorido me pareció apagado. Estos son mis primeros recuerdos de la Escuela de Bellas Artes.

C-LR   ¿ Había ya entonces en Caracas bases documentales, reproducciones, revistas?

JRS   Había únicamente algunas reproducciones, una pequeña biblioteca que contenía documentos sobre historia del arte hasta el impresionismo. Después, mucho más tarde, han llegado algunos libros sobre el cubismo, el "fauvisme," pero yá al fin de mis estudios.

C-LR   ¿ Tuvo Ud. ocasión de ver en aquella época uno o varios cuadros de esos artistas?

JRS   Durante mi útimo año de estudios fuí a ver una colección privada en la cual había, entre otros, cuadros de Sisley y de Dunoyer de Segonzac. Ahí fué donde ví por primera vez obras de pintores. Pero yo no comprendía de veras la orbra impresionista mientras estaba en Venezuela, pues la luz de los impresionistas no tiene relación con la luz tropical, que es muy directa, muy fuerte. Yo me sentí verdaderamente maravillado cuando llegué al alba, por primera vez, a los alrededores de Paris: yo vi los álamos un poco rojizos, pues era ya a comienzos de otoño, y en aquel momento comprendí por qué los impresionistas pintaron tal como lo hicieron.

C-LR En Caracas mientras concluía sus estudios, ¿ seguía Ud. dibujando y pintando para Ud. mismo?

JRS Sí; luego regresé a Ciudad Bolívar para ser profesor, porque la beca me había sido concedida con esa condición, pero no había trabajo para mí allí. En cambio, me llamaron desde Maracaibo para dirigir la pequeña Escuela de Bellas Artes. El alumno más asiduo, allá, era yo; pintaba día y noche, tanto como podía. Nunca pude convencer a mis alumnos de que siguiesen el mismo ritmo, que trabajasen seriamente, a excepción de una joven dama que ha continuado y que hoy es el alma de Maracaibo. Ella conservó esta especie de llama y convirtió a la ciudad al arte moderno.

C-LR ¿Qué pintaba Ud. en esa época, en Maracaibo?

JRS Yo buscaba, a partir del cubismo; pero es evidente que como no tenía ningún elemento acerca de lo que había venido luego, me encontré detenido por mi ignorancia. Sabía que el cubismo se había desarrollado antes de la Primera Guerra y me preguntaba qué había sucedido entre ese período y los años 1948-1950. Habían debido ocurrir cosas formidables que yo no conocía. Yo me decía que no iba a buscar solo, por mí mismo, cosas que seguramente yá estaban hechas, yá habían sido resueltas. . . .

C-LR . . . Al evocar sus comienzos, Ud. hace aparecer de un modo muy natural dos rasgos fundamentales de su carácter que yo he tenido con frecuencia ocasión de encontrar de nuevo en el curso de los trabajos de integración a la arquitectura que Ud. ha proseguido, en relación con mis actividades, durante estos dos últimos años: en primer término, una total falta de interés por los caminos ya trazados y por el contrario una voluntad incontrastable de investigar zonas todavía no exploradas. Por otro lado, una toma de conciencia, aunque no formulada, del inmenso trabajo necesario para llevar a cabo de un modo efectivo esa búsqueda, lo cual exigía una economía de los medios muy severa, evitando abandonarse al diletantismo; un sentido muy preciso de lo que es esencial y de lo que no lo es, a fin de asegurar la supervivencia creadora a los propios ojos de Ud. En el fondo, esta seguridad que Ud. tenía de que había ocurrido en Europa algo que Ud. ignoraba debía serle intolerable; imagino que eso debió contribuír notablemente a su decisión de viajar a París.

JRS   Inclusive, puedo decir que es la única razón, que no hay otra. Yo fuí al lugar donde pensaba encontrar los datos que no conocía. Me puse al corriente muy pronto, y empecé a realizar mis pequeños estudios personales sobre el arte abstracto.

C-LR   En esa época, antes de salir de Venezuela, ¿cómo vivía Soto? Ud. pintaba, Ud. dibujaba casi sin cesar, pero ¿ sentía yá también la misma afición hacia la música? ¿ vivía como ahora, o era Ud. bastante diferente?

JRS   No; verdaderamente, era igual; los amigos que me conocieron en aquella época encuentran que no he cambiado de actitud en absoluto respecto a la gente y a mí mismo.

    Sigue gustándome la música, vivir sin angustia, reunirme con amigos; si puedo organizar una fiesta, lo hago. Yo no mezclo mis sentimientos espontáneos con mi necesidad de elaborar un arte enteramente razonado; son dos cosas que nunca he querido mezclar. Muchas personas han creído vislumbrar una influencia de la música sobre mi obra; es muy posible que ella se encuentre presente, pero en tal caso no se trataría de la música popular que practico sino más bien en el sentido de la música de Bach, a través de su estructura liberada. Pero yo no veo por qué un hombre que sigue una vía muy precisa en una dirección no podría, por otra parte, divertirse como todo el mundo.

C-LR   Me parece que más allá del hombre Soto, a quien vemos abandonarse a las cosas sencillas de la vida, distraerse durante una fiesta, tocar la guitarra, hablar con sus amigos, pasearse, ir al café, hay un hombre más secreto, no ciertamente recóndito en el sentido estricto de la palabra, pero que se protege, se pone a cubierto: dos horas de sueño, tomar rápidamente un avión para cambiar de país, aislarse en un rincón y dejar que los demás hablen entre ellos, llegar inclusive a abstraerse de un ambiente que le gusta para regresar inexorablemente a su trabajo. ¿Es así como Ud. se ve a sí mismo?

JRS   Sí; y no me importa en qué circunstancias, inclusive en una fiesta, si se presenta alguien verdaderamente interesado o interesante en el ámbito del arte tal como yo lo concibo, lo olvido todo y lo abandono todo para consagrarme a lo que, en el fondo, cuenta más para mí. Yo no digo que el resto no me interesa, pero la posibilidad de desarrollar esa gestión a la cual estoy entregado es lo que me sostiene constantemente. Si mi destino hubiera sido el de un científico, yo haría sin duda lo mismo, proseguiría mi investigación en un plano esencialmente especulativo.

C-LR   Esta obstinación ciertamente le ha ayudado a Ud. a adquirir esa cultura muy original, extensa, y de ningún modo libresca ni teórica, muy penetrante, que todo lo pasa por un tamiz sin complacencias. Se tiene la impresión de que en Ud., más allá del exterior sensible, el espíritu crítico está constantemente alerta. Ante cada artista Ud. va a lo esencial, y pregunta: ¿ qué ha aportado? ¿ha hecho avanzar, por poco que sea, la historia del arte, o bien simplemente ha repetido lo ya realizado? ¿es un secuaz, o ha logrado algún progreso en algo?

JRS   Sí; porque de otro modo no hay creación. Si no se hace esto, se hace arte ingenuo. Si no se es un profesional de verdad, si no se concibe el arte como un aporte a la cultura, entonces hay que quedarse en Ciudad Bolívar y hacer arte ingenuo como todo el mundo, como numerosos artistas del mundo. El

arte ingenuo es una manera de expresarse, indudablemente, pero en el fondo, no agrega nada; es
siempre idéntico en todas partes, es más bien un
testimonio de la sensibilidad humana, pero no de la
evolución cultural.

C-LR ¿Cómo definiría Ud. en este campo lo que le parece
nuevo en relación con lo que no es sino repetición?

JRS Es muy sencillo: la historia del arte, la verdadera, la
que me apasiona, la que me interesa, evidentemente
no he sido yo quien la he inventado en el momento
de ponerme en marcha; ella ha sido definida por
una gran cantidad de creadores, de pensadores, es
como un muro que se agranda mediante la super-
posición y la reunión de aportes sucesivos. Otras
posibilidades se presentan sin cesar paralelamente,
y son tal vez motivos de estímulo para los creadores,
pero la más importante es la que continúa directamente la evolución. Es una idea muy positivista, si
Ud. quiere, pero pienso que el arte debe ser positivista. El debe contribuír a la formación de la
sociedad, en un nivel muy profesional; puesto que
nosotros somos artistas formados en el mundo
occidental, con el pensamiento occidental, el arte
debe evolucionar con la misma seriedad, y a la par
que la filosofía, la investigación científica, las
matemáticas, etc. . . . Para mí el arte es valedero
desde el momento en que esta evolución se justifica
racionalmente. . . .

C-LR . . . Ud. sale de Venezuela, y llega a París en 1950;
¿qué es lo primero que encuentra ahí? Naturalmente, suramericanos, amigos, pues yo no lo veo a
Ud. quedarse solo.

JRS No, al contrario. Un grupo de amigos se habían ido
un poco antes que yo, el año anterior; les escribí,
me esperaron, y fueron verdaderamente muy
amables conmigo. Toda la información que ellos
tenían la asimilé inmediatamente. Tomé todos sus
libros y me puse a trabajar hasta las cinco de la
mañana con la ayuda de un diccionario, pues no
conocía ni una palabra de francés. Tres meses
después había leído prácticamente todos esos libros

y tenía todas las informaciones posibles. Me pusieron en relación con el Salón Anual de Réalités Nouvelles y con cuantos artistas ellos conocían en aquella época. Así, junto a Denise René conocí a todos los artistas que, en ese momento, aparecían a mis ojos como investigadores, y tuve ocasión de hablar mucho con ellos. Luego me fuí a ver las obras de Mondrian y de Malevich.

C-LR ¿Dónde las vió Ud.?

JRS Yo pensaba encontrarlas en París; pero como allí no había ninguna, tuve que ir más al norte, hasta Holanda.

C-LR ¿En el Stedelijk Museum y en el Kröller-Müller en Otterlo?

JRS Sí, exactamente.

C-LR Por otra parte, no creo que hubiera muchos libros que trataran de ellos.

JRS No, había sólo algunos artículos; luego, hacia 1954, llegó el primer libro sobre Moholy-Nagy, que estaba en inglés. Lo compré, y encontré una persona benévola, una dama muy intelectual que amable-mente me tradujo dos o tres páginas por noche hasta que leí todo el libro.

C-LR Una vez más, me admira la manera como Ud. se ha ido forjando a sí mismo, solo, paso a paso, como un artesano que en cada ocasión comprueba la calidad de sus materiales y de sus herramientas; y esto sin mostrarlo, dejando creer a los demás que su existencia es fácil, que Ud. se abandona a la buena vida, en tanto que esta despreocupación superficial recubre una inmensa voluntad, absolutamente in-fatigable, de encontrar cueste lo que cueste los elementos de todo tipo indispensables para con-tinuar su formación.

JRS Lo hago plenamente consciente, pues siempre he querido que lo que poseo sea seguro. Si me equivoco, tanto peor; no es que yo busque equivo-carme, pero lo que siempre he querido es que lo poco que poseo lo sienta muy sólido para poder proseguir. Yo sé que hoy tengo una experiencia que es mía, que la poseo muy sólidamente, y esto me permite seguir trabajando. Inclusive si yo no hubiera obtenido cierto éxito, hubiera persistido de la misma manera. Creo que nunca hubiera flaqueado.

C-LR En efecto, Ud. no llegó a ser realmente conocido, más allá del círculo de los amigos, sino alrededor de 1960, después de la Bienal de Venecia, aunque hubiera participado en 1955 en la exposición "El Movimiento" en la Galería Denise René, que agrupaba por primera vez a los principales artistas que trabajaban entonces en direcciones vecinas a la suya. Antes de esto, era el trabajo subterráneo, el túnel; pero Ud. se quedó en París cuando en realidad hubiera podido no permanecer allí e ir a establecerse en otro lugar.
¿Se sentía a gusto en París?

JRS Sí, muy bien.

C-LR ¿Hacia qué se dirigía entonces esencialmente su interés?

JRS En primer lugar, una de las cosas que me impres-ionaron fue una historia relativa a Malevich de una muchacha de Maracaibo que me hablaba despec-tivamente de *Blanco sobre Blanco* del Museum of Modern Art de Nueva York, cuando para mí se ha convertido en una especie de guía espiritual. Y luego, al llegar aquí, vi reproducciones de algunas obras de Kandinsky que empezaban a ser publi-cadas. A mí no me gusta nada el Kandinsky expre-sionista, pero me gusta mucho el Kandinsky "Bauhaus," muy construído. Tomé también con-tacto con la obra de Sophie Tauber, conocí la de Arp y con este bagaje discutí muchísimo con otros artistas y especialmente con mis amigos latinoame-ricanos, cuyo número e importancia son conside-rables. Yo me sentía más bien atraído por las obras que han salido del espíritu "Bauhaus"; y en Klee, por las obras que buscan la perspectiva desde diversos puntos de vista. Esto me ha interesado mucho. Es evidente que dejo a un lado todo el simbolismo de Klee, pero cuando se hace profundo, a mis ojos es una catedral. Descubrí con muchas dificultades la obra de Albers, porque no había casi nada de él aquí. Me informé tanto como pude y finalmente ví sus cuadros en la Galería Denise René cuando ella decidió traerlos y organizar una exposición. He aquí lo que yo recuerdo: Mondrian, Malevich, Klee, Albers, y los amigos con quienes discutía. . . .

C-LR . . . ¿Cómo se desarrollaban sus propios trabajos después de su llegada a París?

JRS En primer lugar, en el período inicial, quise dinamizar las obras de Mondrian, que me gustaban mucho, pues me parecía que se trataba de darles movimiento. No sé por qué lo pensaba así, es un asunto de intuición. Hasta que conocí los *Broadway Boogie-Woogie* y entonces comprendí que Mondrian había resuelto yá ese problema.

C-LR Ud. reaccionaba de nuevo como lo había hecho ante los cubistas: la búsqueda está yá hecha, las soluciones han sido encontradas, no vale la pena perder su tiempo en repeticiones.

JRS Sí, yá que esto estaba terminado, era necesario ir más lejos. Así empezé a escarbar un poco por aquí, un poco por allá. Encontré la vía tomada por Moholy-Nagy muy importante, incompleta indudablemente, a causa de su muerte prematura, pues era uno de los artistas mejor dotados de esa época. Descubrí también a Calder, Marcel Duchamp y Gabo. A partir de la obra de esos creadores comencé a construír un mundo diciéndome que era necesario que yo retomase todos los elementos que ellos habían liberado pero que no habían podido llevar a un término; que yo debía intentar hallar respuestas a todas las preguntas que ellos habían formulado pero no resuelto, a lo que nosotros llamamos en español "planteamientos".

C-LR ¿Preguntas que habían quedado en suspenso? Siempre reaparece el investigador.

JRS Sí, empezé a trabajar para resolver esos problemas no resueltos por otros artistas y finalmente di con el tema de mi verdadero trabajo. Comprendí que había algo que me pertenecía, empezé a desarrollar mi propia vía, conservando el respeto hacia los artistas que me habían guiado.

C-LR ¿Está Ud. de acuerdo en decir que las primeras obras que han concretado esta búsqueda son las *Repeticiones* de 1951?

JRS Sí. La repetición posee un carácter universal, revela estructuras puras, es una ídea básica.

C-LR Se trata, yá, de una desindividualización, de esta desindividualización que se encuentra en la raíz de todos sus trabajos.

JRS Para hacer un arte verdaderamente abstracto -y cuando digo abstracto empleo esta palabra en su pleno significado- es necesario despersonalizarse, es preciso que la situación de cada individuo yá no cuente para nada. Para expansionarme y para canalizar mi vida personal, prefiero reunir a mis amigos, organizar fiestas con ellos, pero no quiero dar a mi trabajo un contenido directamente individual.

C-LR Parece como si toda la riqueza de su vida personal no estuviera ahí sino para permitir que su trabajo surja en condiciones favorables. De manera que en fin de cuentas es el trabajo el que, a pesar de las apariencias, lo ordena todo.

JRS Sí; e inclusive las vacaciones son para mí vacaciones de trabajo. Yo no logro distraerme como todo el mundo en la playa, no es posible. Una hora acostado en la playa dedicado simplemente a olvidarme del mundo, es tiempo perdido. A mí me gusta extraordinariamente el sol, pero debo continuar reflexionando acerca de mi obra.

C-LR Cuántas veces, durante la preparación del proyecto de integración para los nuevos edificios Renault, me ha dicho Ud.: "Recuérdeme cuál es el problema por resolver, pues durante el viaje pensaré en él". Ud. regresaba y a pesar de haber hecho cantidad de cosas, la solución estaba ahí; Ud. había continuado trabajando en su búsqueda sin que se produjera una verdadera interrupción. . . .
La repetición, es la primera despersonalización, es la primera desindividualización, "desanimización," como Ud. lo dice, pero luego Ud. utiliza la progresión que le da mayor énfasis a esta vía.

JRS La repetición es un valor abstracto, que se inscribe perfectamente en lo universal.
La progresión es una variante de la repetición, con un dato no absoluto: el punto de partida. Para universalizarla es preciso concebir la progresión cíclica, en la cual el punto de partida pierde su valor específico.
Luego leí por mi cuenta libros que trataban de la música serial. Yo siempre había sentido una gran admiración por la organización de un mundo fabuloso partiendo de elementos muy simples y abstractos, como en la obra de Bach. Asímismo, descubrir que con la misma serie se podía construír un mundo nuevo me ha impresionado mucho: yo también, hacia 1953, para resolver mi problema, traté de codificar los colores básicos a fin de establecer un sistema serial. A veces me preguntan por qué no he seguido realizando obras "seriales"; simplemente porque la obra serial me condujo rápidamente hacia una nueva etapa, la de las obras vibrantes que se convirtieron en el objetivo de mis búsquedas.

C-LR Sí, un período había terminado. Ud. había encontrado lo que buscaba, partiendo de las repeticiones para llegar a las progresiones y a las obras seriales. . . .
Yo creo, igual que Ud., que no se trata aquí de realizar un análisis teórico de su obra, sino de intentar ofrecer al público precisiones que le permitan situar mejor sus obras a la vez en el contexto de su vida y en relación con los trabajos de sus

contemporáneos o de aquellos cuya importancia Ud. reivindica. Sin embargo ¿ le sería posible a Ud. señalar las principales etapas del desarrollo de su producción a partir de las primeras obras vibrantes?

JRS Las obras seriales salidas de las *Repeticiones* habían dado nacimiento a las vibraciones ópticas del cuadro. Yo pasé casi de inmediato a la super-posición de dos vibraciones, de dos repeticiones, y a las progresiones superpuestas. Y partiendo de estas superposiciones he llegado al movimiento óptico mediante el desplazamiento del espectador ante la obra fija. En primer lugar, son cuadros como *Metamorfosis,* expuesto en Realités Nouvelles en 1954, con una retícula desplazada donde interviene yá el factor tiempo. Despúes hice la *Cajita de Villanueva* con sus tres placas transparentes, rayadas en toda su superficie excepto un cuadrado sin rayas en cada placa: esto creaba una especie de espacio ambiguo y movimientos ópticos. De ahí, pasé a la *Espiral* y a mis otras obras de plexiglás. Yo había trabajado mucho para darme cuenta de la presencia del tiempo en el arte y lograr hacerla perceptible: había descubierto un elemento que debía desarrollar. En ese momento hice no sé yá cuantas obras de plexiglás, muchas de las cuales han desaparecido. Poco a poco, colocando ele-mentos suspendidos libremente entre el plexiglás y el fondo opaco, ambos rayados, me dí cuenta de que sus movimientos podían integrarse a las vibraciones ópticas y llegué así a los objetos suspendidos que Ud. conoce: "curvas inmateriales", varillas, etc. . . . que, mediante el juego de los desplazamientos, desaparecen para no formar yá sino vibraciones.

C-LR A partir de los plexiglás resultaba evidente que la obra de arte, tal como Ud. la concebía, aun cuando, naturalmente, en su origen era siempre creación de Ud. no podía existir sin la participación activa del espectador, quien por su movimiento hacía aparecer las vibraciones que Ud. había introducido en ella. Y Ud., no podía existir sin la participación activa del desempeñe de este papel en todas las obras si-guientes. Esta participación del espectador, así como la desindividualización y la universalización, era in-separable, a partir de ese momento, de su trabajo.

JRS Continué así durante casi dos años, y descubrí la infinidad de posibilidades que me ofrecía la super-posición de dos superficies entramadas. Yo tenía conciencia de estar buscando valores para construír algo más adelante, pero me daba cuenta de que eran elementos todavía no controlados totalmente por mí; ellos permanecían casi demasiado completa-mente libres.

C-LR Ud, estaba domesticando algo nuevo.

JRS Mire. En un momento dado comprendí que debía eliminar una de las dos libertades y es así como, a partir de 1957, conservé simplemente la trama del fondo, muy apretada, casi mecánica y dejé en libertad a la parte superpuesta. De ese modo llegué a la etapa casa barroca que Ud. conoce, con ma-teriales heteróclitos, a fin de probarme a mí mismo que cualquier elemento era válido para esto. Cuando comprendí que todo era posible, me puse de nuevo a controlar esos elementos y escogí los que eran más simples, los que se adaptaban mejor a mi propósito.

C-LR Para traducir esta universalidad, Ud. apela a los medios materiales más simples, con un propósito de economía y de eficacia que nunca le abandona.

JRS Ud. sabe, vengo de un país, Venezuela, donde cuando yo era joven todo estaba por hacer, y para hacerlo uno no podía contar sino con sus propios medios. Ya se lo he dicho: busqué hasta encontrar exactamente lo que quería, y poco a poco adquirí, gracias a mi trabajo, un lenguaje que me permitiera mostrar mis descubrimientos.

C-LR En todas las retrospectivas de obras suyas que he visto en Europa me ha impresionado siempre la evidencia de un éxito realmente maravilloso, y tanto más maravilloso por haberse renovado en varias ocasiones de manera distinta mediante diferentes series: un éxito que consiste en alcanzar, para cada problema planteado, la solución más directa, la más pura, haciendo que los elementos más simples sean capaces de transmitir exactamente los fenómenos que Ud. había aislado y que Ud. quería hacer percibir.

JRS Quiero trabajar hasta que lo logre, pues tengo em-peño en esta economía de medios.

C-LR Para mí, las obras que se sucedieron de 1962 a 1967, las *Curvas Inmateriales,* con sus varillas de metal horizontales idénticas, suspendidas por hilos de nylon ante una superficie de trama uniforme, los *cuadrados vibrantes,* las *varillas suspendidas para-lelas,* y más recientemente, las *Tes,* cristalizan los hitos de los descubrimientos hechos por Ud. en su carrera, y yá han alcanzado una perfección defini-tiva. Y nosotros volveremos a encontrar más ade-lante esta misma cualidad, esta misma nitidez en el propósito, con sus obras inscritas en un espacio más vasto, bien se trate de los *Penetrables,* o de las *Ex-tensiones* y de las *Progresiones en el suelo* a partir de 1968.

En cuanto a mí, pongo a parte ciertas obras hacia las cuales, como Ud. sabe, me siento particular-mente atraído : las que Ud. llama *Escrituras.* En cierto modo se puede encontrar ahí, creo yo, como un regreso singular al rasgo directo de la mano del artista, y tal vez hay también, aun manteniéndose coherente con su voluntad de desindividualización, una transcripción más inmediata de su sensibilidad personal, como un permiso más o menos con-scientemente concedido a su mano para actuar con mayor libertad. Entramos ahí en un ámbito bastante secreto, cada vez redescubierto, como si asistiéra-mos a algo indiscreto en relación con el resto de su obra.

JRS Es posible. Las *Escrituras* son para mí una manera de dibujar en el espacio.

Cruz Diez, con quien estudié, me dijo ante las primeras *Escrituras:* "Es tu idioma, son los mismos signos, lo mismo que cuando tú quisiste ir más allá de Mondrian." Es verdad, yo no había siquiera pen-sado en esto. Era también con curvas así como esta-ban dibujados mis paisajes. Es muy posible que si yo hubiera sido un pintor del siglo XVIII, mi mano hubiera dibujado instintivamente con rasgos análogos. Tal vez . . . Pero inclusive dentro de esta libertad, yo sigo, como Ud. ve, conservando la estructura, controlando de todos modos los elementos.

C-LR Parece como si el desfase entre la trama impersonal del fondo y las varillas dobladas o curvadas al arbitrio de su libertad, le hubiera permitido a Ud. crear ahí un lenguaje capaz de encerrar el máximo de individualidad compatible con su voluntad de universalidad. Inclusive en estas *Escrituras* las vibraciones puras están lejos de hallarse ausentes, y nacen de las varillas verticales que fluctúan al ritmo de las curvas y de las líneas quebradas.

De todas maneras, estas incursiones furtivas de una mano que no traduce, por otra parte, el "statement" de Ud., son escasas, y no le han arrastrado nunca fuera de su propio territorio.

JRS No, yo he seguido trabajando siempre en la misma dirección, y estas "escrituras" se han intercalado de manera intermitente entre búsquedas más rigurosas y más controladas.

C-LR ¿ Cómo reaccionaba Ud. ante los trabajos de artistas que habían tomado direcciones completamente distintas de las suyas? ¿ sequía Ud. sus trabajos? Es ciertamente uno de los rasgos más característicos de nuestra época, que concepciones aparentemente opuestas de un modo radical, situadas en órbitas muy alejadas una de otra, pueden coexistir y proseguir cada una su destino sin interferencias. Así, a medida que Ud. alcanza una despersonalización y una universalidad poniendo en vigencia la estructura de la materia original, otros artistas rehusan por el contrario perder cualquier parcela de su individualidad. Dubuffet, por ejemplo, se empeña en captar el bullir de la vida constituída, desde lo orgánico más o menos indiferenciado hasta lo que surge de los aspectos más abruptos de lo imaginario.

JRS Sí, es un camino completamente distinto, pero yo lo respeto . . . .

. . . Regresemos a su obra de 1968; Ud., pues, mediante experiencias sucesivas, delimitó el campo de sus búsquedas. Ud. llevó hasta su última y más evidente expresión las preocupaciones que le habían mantenido en suspenso durante más de 15 años, y Ud. es el autor de una obra coherente que ocupa yá un lugar fundamental en la evolución del arte contemporáneo. Me parece, de todos modos, que los años 1968 y 1969 constituyen de nuevo para Ud. un momento importante por tres tipos de razones: en primer lugar, Ud. dispone de medios materiales que no tienen común medida con los que tenía en sus comienzos, lo cual le permite liberarse y realizar obras a una escala mucho más vasta como el *Cubo de Espacio Ambiguo* o los largos alineamientos rectos o curvados de varillas verticales cuyas dimensiones son las mismas de la Sala en la cual son colocados. La relación de la obra con el espectador se acentúa y cambia entonces, inclusive, de naturaleza: éste participaba en la obra que se encontraba frente a él, y ahora ese espectador y el espacio que Ud. ha llenado se convierten en indisolubles. Este revolucionario aporte se hará más brillante con su creación de los *Penetrables,* en los cuales el espectador se introduce entre los hilos o las varillas verticales que han invadido todo el volumen disponible y constituyen la obra misma, animándolos; así, pues, desde ese momento obra y espectador se hallan físicamente mezclados de un modo inextricable. Con esos *Penetrables,* Ud. llega a materializar totalmente su sentimiento profundo de la situación del hombre inmerso en un universo "lleno," en el cual materia, espacio y tiempo no son sino uno en un "continuum" de vibraciones infinitas. Finalmente, y tal es sin duda el aspecto más actual de su actividad artística, Ud. concede a partir de ese momento un lugar de primer plano a sus trabajos de integración a la arquitectura, los cuales hacen que su obra salga del medio especializado para unirla directamente a la vida cotidiana de sus contemporáneos. Esta voluntad de poner al alcance de los demás sus descubrimientos lo conduce a aceptar las imposiciones inherentes a todas esas integraciones realizadas hoy, es decir, en un marco concebido por hombres que muy frecuentemente están en retraso en relación a investigaciones como las que Ud. adelanta.

JRS   Yo las acepto. No es tiempo perdido. Es un trabajo que significa mucho para mí. Yo no veo por qué rehusaría adaptarme a una situación que es lo que es. Lamentablemente, yo empiezo a trabajar cuando los proyectos están yá muy avanzados, puesto que nuestra sociedad se halla todavía en un estado que no le permite concebir de otra manera nuestro trabajo. Es un esfuerzo suplementario. Aguardo tranquilamente las maquetas y hago lo que puedo para intervenir, haciendo las menos concesiones posibles. Creo que la gente que pasará todos los días por el nuevo salón de entrada de las Fábricas Renault, por ejemplo, entre las columnas entramadas, los bloques de cuadrados vibrantes y la gran *Escritura* de 30 metros de largo que se reunirá al plafón formado por 250.000 varillas suspendidas encima de ellos, descubrirán algo que estaba en ellos mismo pero de lo cual todavía no tenían conocimiento.

   Los *Penetrables,* las nuevás extensiones en el suelo, las integraciones a la arquitectura, son, en el fondo, el punto de conjunción de todas mis búsquedas anteriores. Yo he trabajado siempre como investigador que desea encontrar algo: como la obra serial me había conducido a la vibración óptica del cuadro y las superposiciones me habían llevado a las obras que realmente están en movimiento, la búsqueda de un lenguaje universal, hecho de frases-tipo, de elementos de mostrativos, me ha llevado naturalmente hacia la abstracción pura. Con mi ídea del universal, no hay yá limitación en cuanto a la medida: yo podría hacer una obra que fuera desde París al Havre, o que atravesara el océano, y sería el mismo concepto. Simplemente, lo que ocurre es que durante mucho tiempo no pude hacer sino pequeñas obras de laboratorio. Pero para mí es idéntica la realización de un cuadro que yo llamaría más bien una obra de taller, y la creación de una obra cuya escala es ilimitada. Yo sigo buscando. Pienso que el arte es una ciencia, una forma de ciencia.

C-LR Ud. dice con frecuencia que el arte es la ciencia de aquello que no puede probarse de otro modo.

JRS Exactamente. Esta es mi opinión, que expresé yá cuando realicé mi exposición en el Stedelijk Museum de Amsterdam: "lo inmaterial es la realidad sensible del universo. El arte es el conocimiento sensible de lo inmaterial. Tomar conciencia de lo inmaterial el estado de estructura pura, es franquear la última etapa hacia lo absoluto."
Yo no concibo al arte de otro modo, y cuando se piensa así se alcanza un mundo fabuloso que nunca ha sido explorado. Por esta razón, cuando oigo decir que el arte abstracto ha muerto (yá lo decían hacia 1950) quienes tal cosa afirman me hacen reir.

C-LR Ud. dice también con frecuencia que Ud. no se sentiría satisfecho si descubriera únicamente unos fenómenos y se quedara en eso. Ud. tiene necesidad de comunicarlos a los demás, pues le interesan sus reacciones.

JRS Si yo continúo ejecutando obras de arte, es precisamente para demostrar a los demás esos fenómenos que he descubierto yá. Personalmente, como lo he dicho en otras ocasiones, podria abstenerme de seguir haciéndolas, pero quiero despertar a la gente e interesarlos en el conocimiento de fenómenos universales que al artista, el sabio, el filósofo, presienten . . . .

C-LR . . . De su vida, de su trabajo, así como de todo lo que Ud. dice, se desprende un respeto profundo y serio por la creación artística, a la vez como medio de conocer el mundo y como medio de comunicación con los demás. Ud. no se encierra en un aislamiento egoista, y paga el precio de las responsabilidades sociales que asume.
Ud. ha escogido actuar a través de la obra de arte misma, aun cuando al mismo tiempo tenga que metamorfosearla completamente a fin de hacerla compatible con el marco retardatario de nuestra

vida. Hay en Ud. una creencia optimista en la obra que está por construír, en su permanencia misma, mientras que otros quieren orientarse hacia lo efímero, la intervención espontánea y en fin de cuentas hacia una negación de la obra misma.

JRS Mire; al principio me interesé también por la obra efímera porque me parecía un medio de captar el carácter universal de un momento. Pero yo la abandoné cuando comprendí que inclusive las cosas efímeras que construía no lo eran nunca verdaderamente. La gente encontraba siempre la manera, de un modo o de otro, de reconstruirlas; e inclusive, si no podian reconstruírlas, las obras quedaban inmovilizadas en su mente.

C-LR Por otra parte, entiendo que su actitud es también muy clara en lo que concierne a las relaciones del arte y la política. Ud. no es de aquellos que mezclan directamente sus búsquedas con las posiciones que puedan tener a este respecto.

JRS Sí, yo separo el arte de la política, porque considero que la política es una serie de etapas transitorias, y que si someto a ella mi trabajo, éste perderá la solidez que le he dado, me desviaré de mi concepto especulativo, abandonaré poco a poco mis búsquedas en tanto que artista en beneficio de las necesidades políticas. En la sociedad el arte es tan importante como la política. Me parece normal que el político dé prioridad a la política; pero, yo, como artista, pienso que debo dar prioridad al arte.

C-LR Desde hace varios años Ud. ha contestado con actos a quienes pasan su tiempo debatiendo el papel social del artista. Así, Ud. ha consagrado buena parte de su tiempo, de sus fuerzas y de su dinero a crear al Museo de Arte Contemporáneo de Ciudad Bolívar, para el cual Ud. ha proporcionado lo esencial de las obras, no únicamente las suyas, sino también las de otros artistas. Me conmueve el hecho de que un artista yá célebre, pero que tiene todavía la mitad de su vida activa ante sí, dedique tantos esfuerzos a ese Museo en lugar de aprovecharse por fin de una libertad tan duramente adquirida.

JRS Yo no he olvidado nunca las dificultades que tuve para descubrir y comprender el arte. A través del Museo de Ciudad Bolívar, quisiera informar a los jóvenes a fin de evitarles las mismas dificultades. Si pudiera ofrecerles esto, me sentiría yá muy feliz.

La razón que me ha inducido a llevar a cabo un esfuerzo tan grande ha sido la de crear en su totalidad en la población donde en mis comienzos tuve que luchar tanto, algo que pueda servir de punto de partida a quienes se interesan por esos temas. Si logro esto, aun cuando sea tan solo para dos o tres artistas que saldrán de ahí en el porvenir, me sentiré muy contento, habré ganado la partida. Y si no hay artistas, ese Museo habrá servido para informar a la gente de Ciudad Bolívar y de los otros lugares de los alrededores que empiezan a visitarlo. Se trata simplemente de una voluntad pedagógica, y de la certidumbre de que frente a los fenómenos universales las reacciones de un hombre de un país llamado subdesarrollado y las de un país llamado superdesarrollado son idénticas.

No olivide Ud., aún cuando las cosas hayan evolucionado mucho actualmente, que provengo de un país que, cuando salí de él por primera vez, era más bien considerado como muy poco desarrollado. Yo pertenezco a un país que todavía no ha construído su mundo. Para nosotros no se trata de destruir. Comprendo muy bien que un país como Alemania cree el arte expresionista, o que los Estados Unidos, que han alcanzado un alto nivel de vida, quieran hacer marcha atrás y regresar a las fuentes; o que en Francia o en Italia la gente se pregunte si hay que replantear la búsqueda de la felicidad. Nosotros todavía no hemos alcanzado esa felicidad: eso es lo que primero debemos lograr. Después, podremos tratar de averiguar si tenemos tal vez que rasgar algo, para despertarnos de esa felicidad.

Por ahora, no hemos llegado a ese punto; tenemos que construír, ante todo, esta felicidad, debemos crearla y conquistarla . . .

1
Optical Repetition No. 2. 1951
Répétition optique No. 2
Repetición Optica No. 2

Wood and enamel, 74⅞ x 51⅜ x 1″

Collection Museo de Arte Moderno "Jesús Soto,"
Ciudad Bolivar, Venezuela

Works in the Exhibition

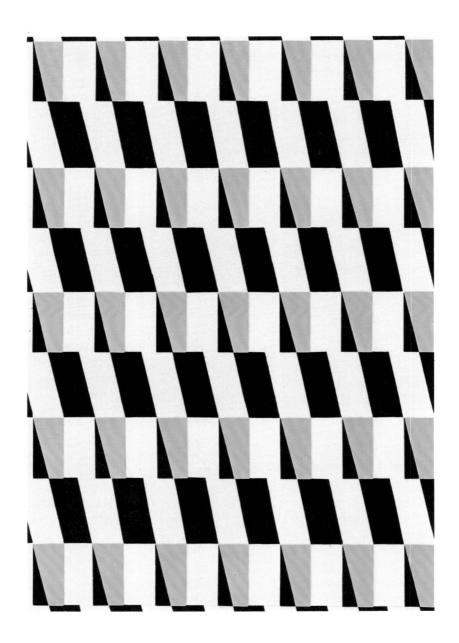

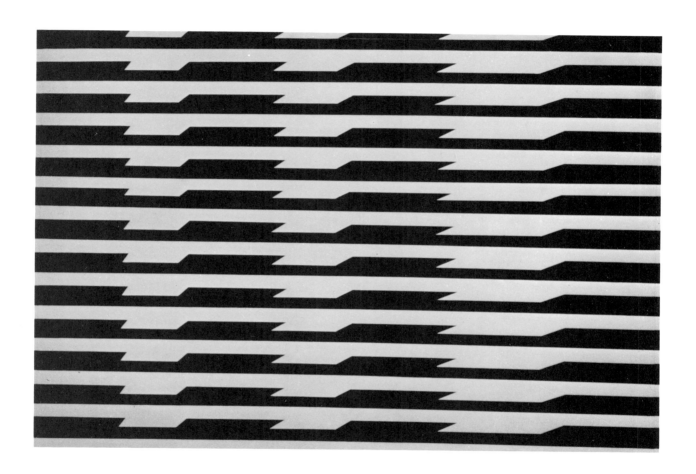

2
Repetition and Progression. 1951
Répétition et progression
Repetición y Progressión

Cardboard, enamel and wood, 51⅜ x 75 x ⅞ "

Collection Museo de Arte Moderno "Jesús Soto,"
Ciudad Bolivar, Venezuela

3
Interfering Parallels Black and White. 1951-52
Parallèles interférentes noires et blanches
Paralelas Interferentes Negras y Blancas

Plaka and wood, 47¼ x 47 x 2"

Collection Museo de Arte Moderno "Jesús Soto,"
Ciudad Bolivar, Venezuela

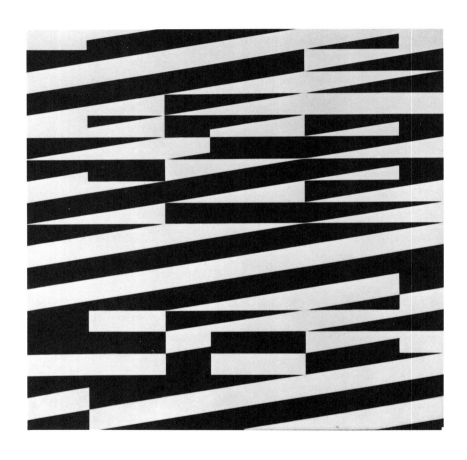

4
Rotation. 1952
Rotation
Rotación

Wood and plaka, 39½ x 39½ x 3″

Collection Museo de Arte Moderno "Jesús Soto,"
Ciudad Bolivar, Venezuela

5
Progression. 1952
Progression
Progresión

Wood and plaka, 40¼ x 40¼ x 2¾"

Collection Museo de Arte Moderno "Jesús Soto,"
Ciudad Bolivar, Venezuela

6
Study for a Series. 1952-53
Etude pour une série
Estudio para una Serie

Wood, paper and enamel, 40¼ x 40¼ x 2⅜″

Collection Museo de Arte Moderno "Jesús Soto,"
Ciudad Bolivar, Venezuela

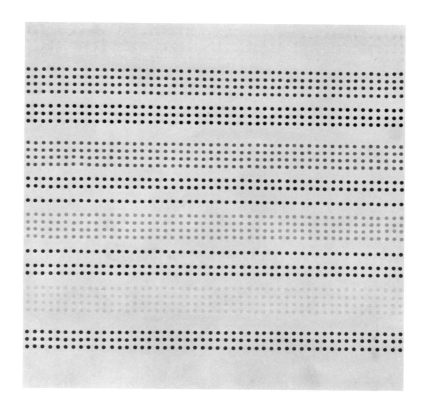

7
Serial Painting. 1952-53
Tableau sérial
Pintura Serial
Wood and enamel, 39½ x 39⅜ x 2⅝ "
Collection José Hoffman

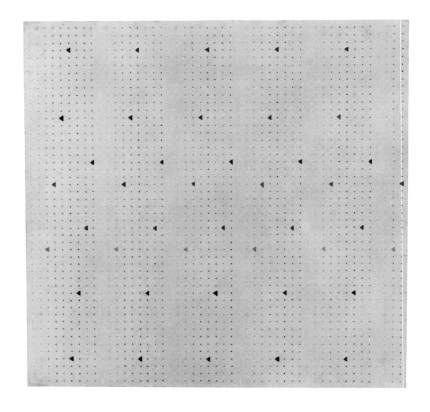

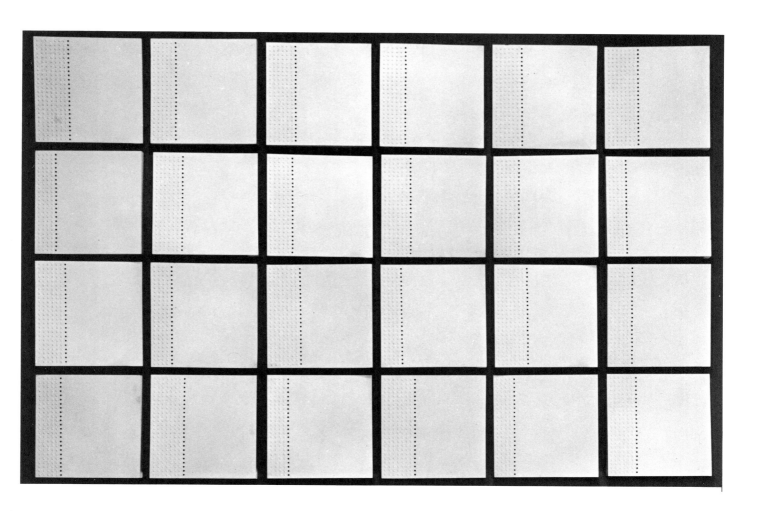

8
White Wall. 1952-53
Mur blanc
Muro Blanco

Wood, paperboard and paint, 82¾ x 126"

Collection Museo de Arte Moderno "Jesús Soto,"
Ciudad Bolivar, Venezuela

9
Two Squares in Space. 1953
Deux carrés dans l'espace
Dos Cuadrados en el Espacio

Wood, enamel and plexiglas, 14 x 24½ x 3″

Collection Museo de Arte Moderno "Jesús Soto,"
Ciudad Bolivar, Venezuela

10
Evolution. 1953
Evolution
Evolución

Wood, paper and plexiglas, 39¼ x 39¼ ″

Collection Kaiser Wilhelm Museum, Krefeld,
Germany

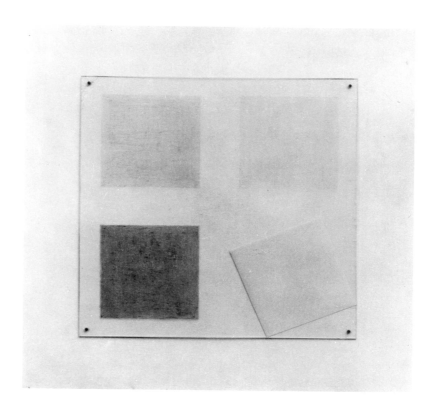

11
Displacement of a Transparent Square. 1953-54
Déplacement d'un carré transparent
Desplazamiento de un Cuadrado Transparente

Wood, plaka and enamel, 39½ x 39½ x 1 ½ "

Dr. and Mrs. Carlos Raul Villanueva Collection, Caracas

12

White Points over Black Points. 1954
Points blancs sur points noirs
Puntos Blancos sobre Puntos Negros

Plexiglas, wood and enamel, 39½ x 39½ x 6″

Dr. and Mrs. Carlos Raul Villanueva Collection,
Caracas

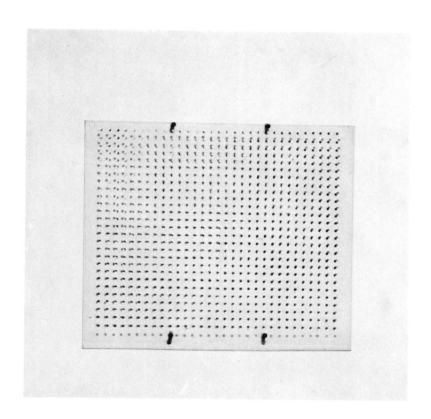

13
Metamorphosis. 1954
Métamorphose
Metamorfosis

Plexiglas, wood and enamel, 39½ x 39½ x 1¾ ″

Collection Museo de Arte Moderno "Jesús Soto,"
Ciudad Bolivar, Venezuela

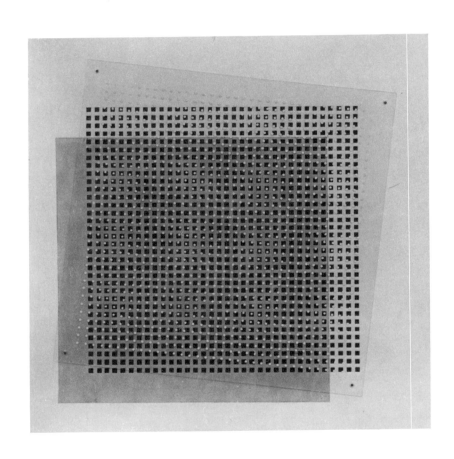

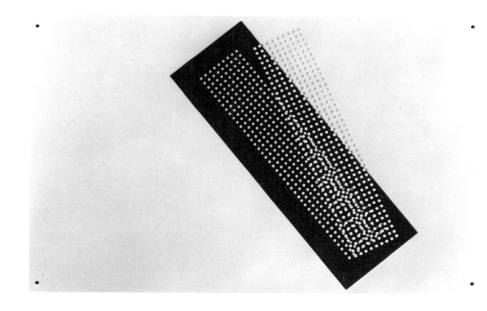

14
Displacement of a Luminous Element. 1954
Déplacement d'un élément lumineux
Desplazamiento de un Elemento Luminoso
Wood, paint and plexiglas, 19¾ x 31½ x 1″
Collection Lya Imber de Coronil

15
Metamorphosis of a Square. 1955
Métamorphose d'un carré
Metamorfosis de un Cuadrado

Plexiglas, wood, metal and enamel,
39⅜ x 39¼ x 3¼"

Dr. and Mrs. Carlos Raul Villanueva Collection,
Caracas

16
Three-Six-Nine. 1955
Trois-six-neuf
Tres-Seis-Nueve

Plexiglas, wood and paint, 39½ x 39½ x 3¼ ″

Dr. and Mrs. Carlos Raul Villanueva Collection,
Caracas

17
The Little Villanueva Box. 1955
La petite boîte de Villanueva
La Cajita de Villanueva
Plexiglas and paint, 12 x 12 x 4″
Dr. and Mrs. Carlos Raul Villanueva Collection,
Caracas

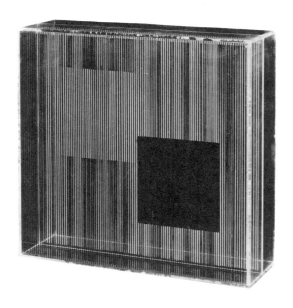

18

Spiral with Red. 1955
Spirale avec rouge
Espiral con Rojo

Plexiglas, wood and enamel, 21 x 20¾ x 10¼ "

Dr. and Mrs. Carlos Raul Villanueva Collection, Caracas

19

Kinetic Structure of Geometric Elements. 1955
Structure cinétique à éléments géométriques
Estructura Cinética de Elementos Geométricos

Plexiglas, wood and paint, 19¾ x 19¾ x 10¼ "

Collection Inocente Palacios

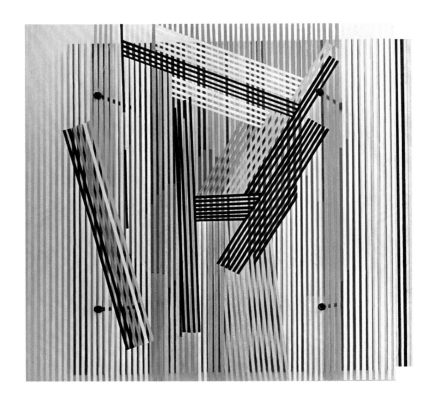

20
Kinetic Structure of Geometric Elements. 1955
Structure cinétique à éléments géométriques
Estructura Cinética de Elementos Geométricos

Wood, paint and plexiglas, 29¼ x 29⅜ x 12¾″

Dr. and Mrs. Carlos Raul Villanueva Collection,
Caracas

21
Kinetic Structure of Geometric Elements. 1956
Structure cinétique à éléments géométriques
Estructura Cinética de Elementos Geométricos
Plexiglas, wood and plaka, 37½ x 37½ x 12½ ″
Collection Museo de Bellas Artes, Caracas

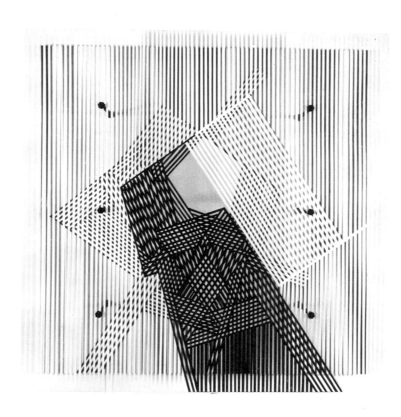

22
Permutation. 1956
Permutation
Permutación

Wood, plaka, metal and plexiglas, 15¾ x 15¾ x 9″

Collection Museo de Arte Moderno "Jesús Soto,"
Ciudad Bolivar, Venezuela

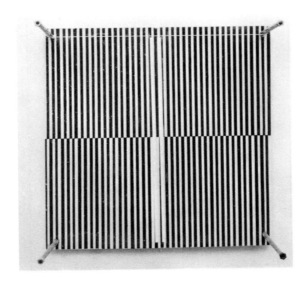

23
Silver Light. 1956
Lumière argentée
Luz Plateada

Plexiglas, wood and plaka, 39½ x 39½ x 13¼ "

Dr. and Mrs. Carlos Raul Villanueva Collection,
Caracas

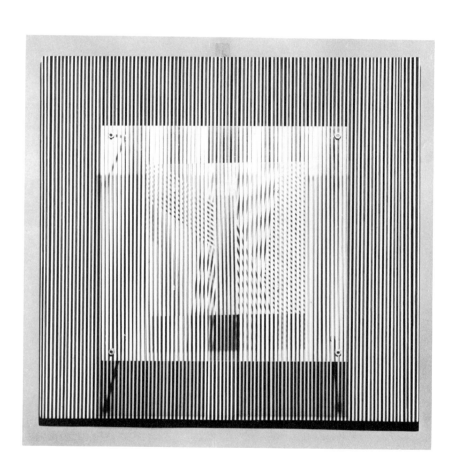

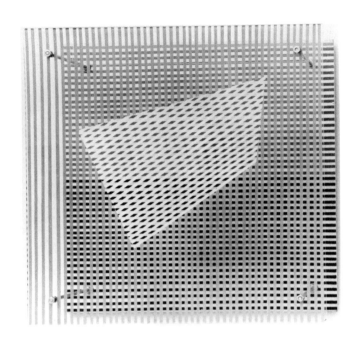

24
*Kinetic Structure of Geometric Elements. The
Trapeze.* 1957
*Structure cinétique à éléments géométriques. Le
trapèze*
*Estructura Cinética de Elementos Geométricos. El
Trapecio*

Wood, plaka and plexiglas, 23 x 23 x 9¾ ″

Collection Museo de Arte Moderno "Jesús Soto,"
Ciudad Bolivar, Venezuela

25
Kinetic Structure. 1957
Structure cinétique
Estructura Cinética

Wood, plexiglas, enamel and plaka,
60 x 60¼ x 10¼ "

Collection Museo de Arte Moderno "Jesús Soto,"
Ciudad Bolivar, Venezuela

26
Pre-penetrable. 1957
Pré-pénétrable
Pre-penetrable
Iron and paint, 65½ x 49½ x 33½ ″
Collection Alfredo and Yolanda Boulton

29
Metallic Vibration. 1961
Vibration métallique
Vibración Metálica

Wood, paint and metal, 23¾ x 23¾ x 11½ ″
Collection Milada S. Neumann, Caracas

27
Spiral. 1958
Spirale
Espiral

Plexiglas, wood and paint, 19⅞ x 19⅞ x 9½ "

Dr. and Mrs. Carlos Raul Villanueva Collection,
Caracas

28
First Vibrating Square. 1958
Premier carré vibrant
Primer Cuadrado Vibrante

Metal, wood and paint, 23¾ x 23¾ x 7"

Lent by the artist

30
Ambiguous Cubes. 1961
Cubes ambigus
Cubos Ambiguos

Wood, metal, paint and pasteboard,
39½ x 39½ x 10⅛″

Collection Museo de Bellas Artes, Caracas

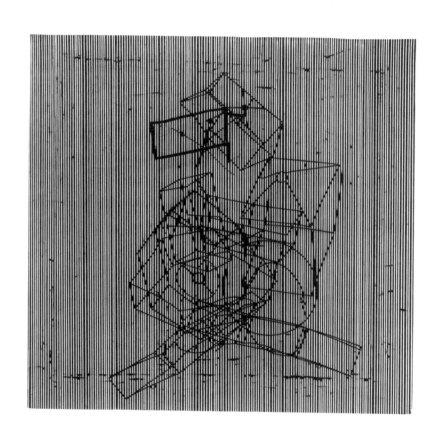

31
Grains of Rubber. 1961
Colles granulées
Puntos de Goma

Metal, wood, burlap, pasteboard and lime,
28½ x 28½ x 6″

Collection Alfredo and Yolanda Boulton

32
Black Baroque. 1961
Baroque noir
Barroco Negro
Wire, pasteboard, burlap and paint, 37½ x 62½ x 6″
Collection Alfredo and Yolanda Boulton

33
Plexiglas Box. 1962
La boîte en plexiglas
La Cajita de Plexiglas

Wood, enamel and plexiglas, 16 x 23¾ x 4½″

Collection Museo de Arte Moderno "Jesús Soto,"
Ciudad Bolivar, Venezuela

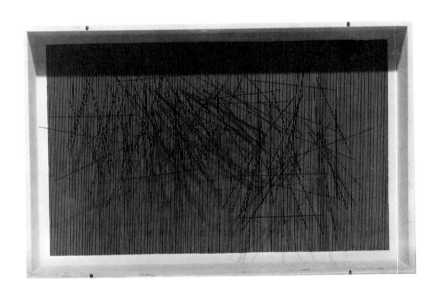

34
The Little Metal Box. 1962
La petite boîte métallique
La Cajita Metálica

Paint, metal, masonite and wood, 13¾ x 15⅜ x 3¾ ″

Collection Milada S. Neumann, Caracas

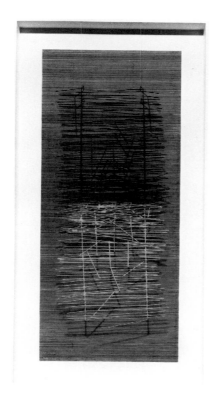

35
The Ladder. 1962
L'Echelle
La Escalera

Wood, metal, nylon cord and paint, 40 x 20½ x 4″

Lent by the artist

36
Vibration. 1963
Vibration
Vibración
Metal, wood, paint and nylon cord, 50 x 41 x 6¼ ″
Collection Museo de Bellas Artes, Caracas

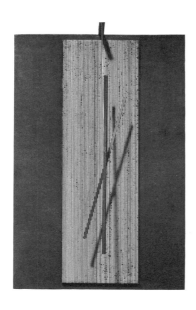

37
The Dialogue. 1963
Le Dialogue
El Dialogo

Metal, wood, paint and nylon cord, 9¾ x 15¼ x 4¼ ″

Lent by the artist

38
Relation-Vibration. 1964
Relation-vibration
Relación-Vibración

Wood, metal and plaka, 42½ x 41¾ x 6″

Collection Museo de Arte Moderno ''Jesús Soto,''
Ciudad Bolivar, Venezuela

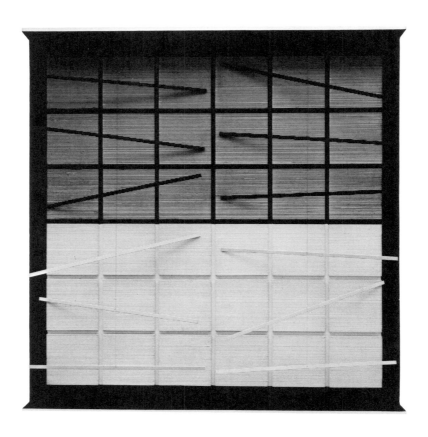

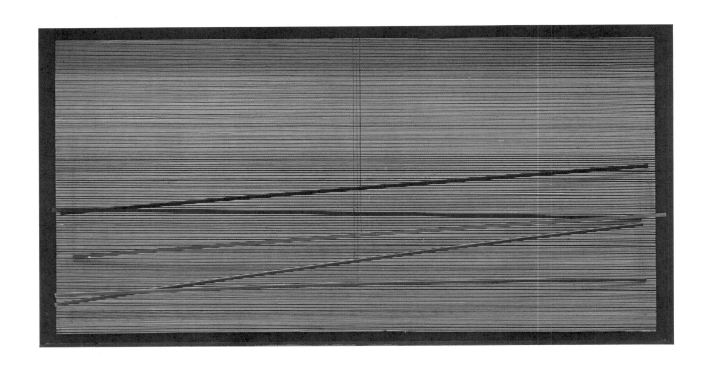

39
Five Big Rods. 1964
Cinq grandes tiges
Cinco Grandes Varillas

Metal, wood and paint, 36¼ x 68½ x 6⅜ ″

Collection Museo de Arte Moderno ''Jesús Soto,''
Ciudad Bolivar, Venezuela

40

Opposed Movements: White and Black. 1965
Mouvements opposés: Blanc et noir
Movimientos Opuestos: Blanco y Negro

Wood, paint and metal, 22½ x 13 x 5¾ "

Lent by the artist

41
Vibrating Columns. 1965
Colonnes vibrantes
Columnas Vibrantes
Metal, wood, paint and nylon cord, 81⅜ x 42 x 15½ ″
Collection José Rafael Viso

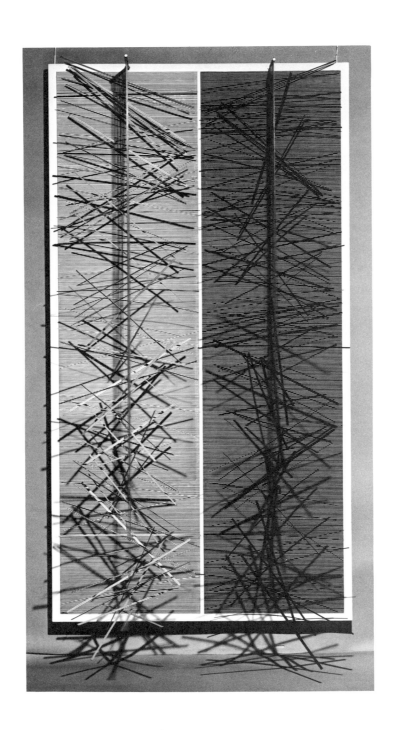

42
Three Squares with Red. 1955
Trois carrés avec rouge
Tres Cuadrados con Rojo

Wood, metal and enamel, 26½ x 26⅞ x 6″

Collection Museo de Arte Moderno ''Jesús Soto,''
Ciudad Bolivar, Venezuela

43
Sixteen Vibrating Red and Black Squares. 1965
Seize carrés vibrants rouges et noirs
Dieciséis Cuadrados Vibrantes Rojos y Negros

Wood, plaka and pasteboard, 42½ x 42⅝ x 6¼ ″

Collection Roger Boulton

44
Horizontal Vibration. 1965
Vibration horizontale
Vibración Horizontal

Wood, metal, nylon and plaka, 27 x 74 x 8″

Collection Alfredo and Yolanda Boulton

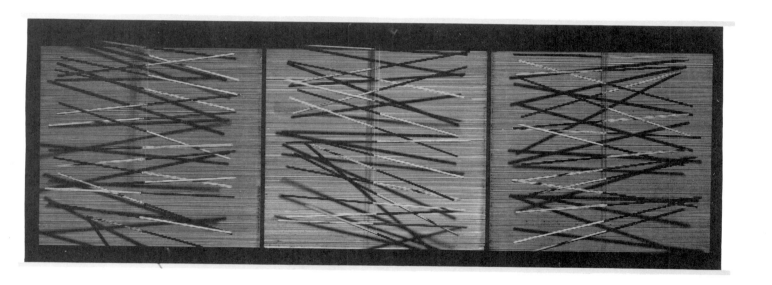

45
Vibration. 1965
Vibration
Vibración

Metal, wood and oil, 62⅜ x 42¼ x 5¾ ″

Collection The Solomon R. Guggenheim Museum,
New York

Gift Eve Clendenin, 1967

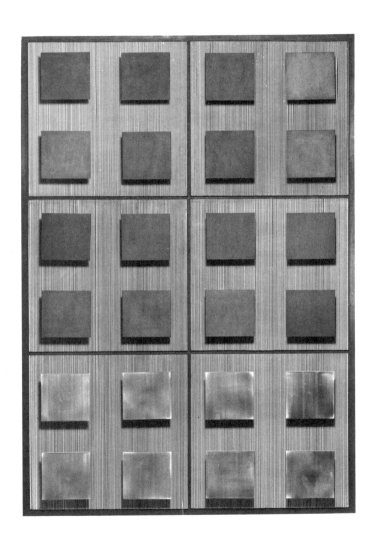

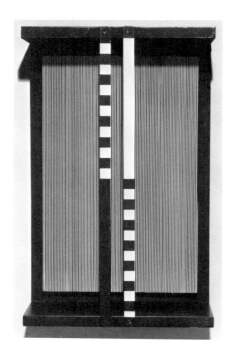

46
Two Vertical Positions. 1966
Deux positions verticales
Dos Posiciónes Verticales

Wood, metal and paint, 19 x 11⅝ x 5½ ″

Collection William and Sylvia Ellis

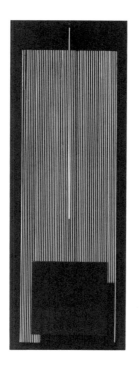

47
Three Speeds. 1966
Trois vitesses
Tres Velocidades

Wood, metal and paint, 19 x 6¾ x 5″

Lent by the artist

48
Immaterial Curves: Brown and Black. 1966
Courbes immaterielles: Marrons et noirs
Curvas Inmateriales: Marrones y Negras
Nylon, metal, wood and plaka, 61⅜ x 41¼ x 15⅛ ″
Collection Inocente Palacios

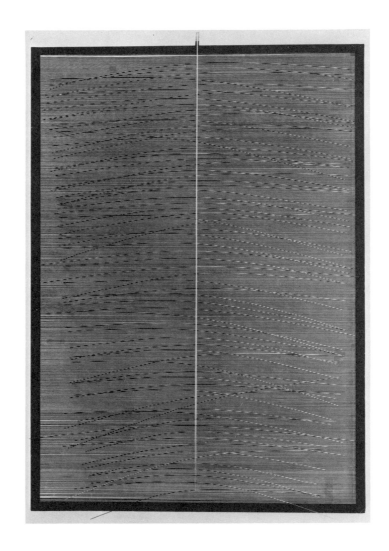

49
White over Black. 1966
Blanc sur noir
Blanco sobre Negro

Wood, wire, paint and nylon cord, 62 x 42½ x 8¾ "

Collection Emanuel Hoffman-Fondation,
Kunstmuseum Basel

50
Big White. 1966
Grand blanc
Grand Blanco
Wood, wire, paint and nylon cord, 82 x 61 x 13"
Lent by Galerie Denise René, Paris, New York

51
Black, Silver and Yellow Relation. 1966
Relation noir, argent et jaune
Relación Negro, Plata y Amarillo

Wood, metal and plaka, 62¼ x 82½ x 6″

Collection Museo de Arte Moderno "Jesús Soto,"
Ciudad Bolivar, Venezuela

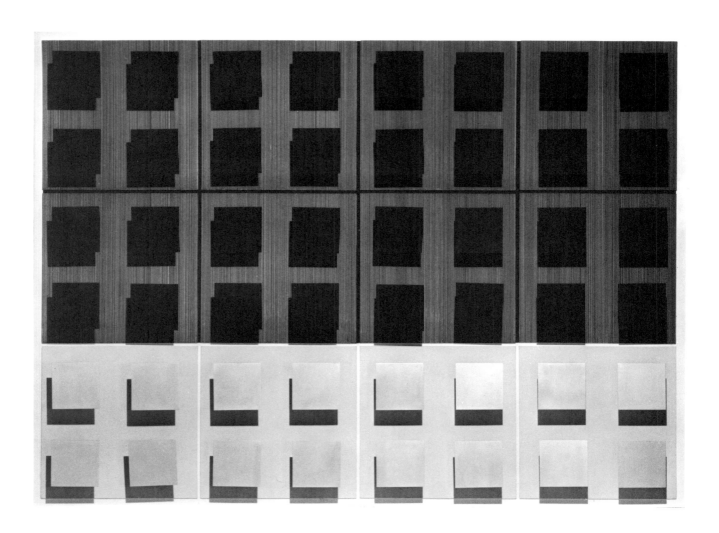

52
Double Writing: Black and Green. 1966
Ecriture double: Noir et verte
Doble Escritura: Negra y Verde

Metal, wood, pasteboard and paint, 43 x 68 x 7⅛ ″

Lent by Galeria Conkright, Caracas

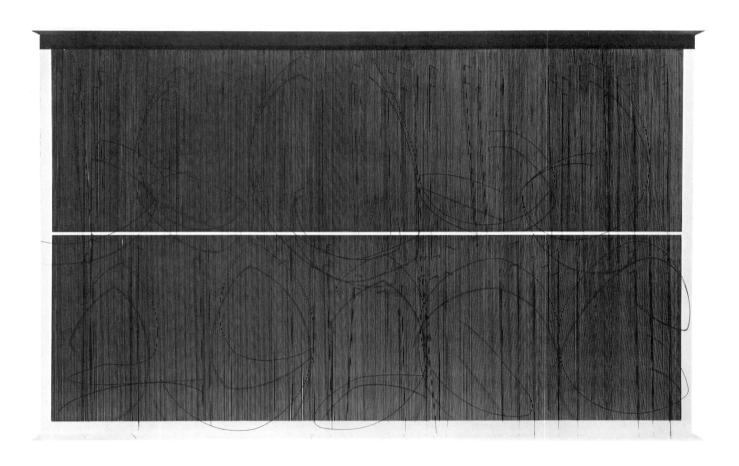

53
Two Virtual Relations. 1967
Deux relations virtuelles
Dos Relaciones Virtuales

Wood, metal, nylon, enamel and cardboard,
41¾ x 22 x 9⅜″

Collection Museo de Arte Moderno "Jesús Soto,"
Ciudad Bolivar, Venezuela

54
Salon de Mai 67. 1967
Salon de Mai 67
Salon de Mai 67

Wood, wire, paint, nylon cord and metal,
61¾ x 81½ x 12¾ ″

Lent by Galerie Denise René, Paris, New York

55
Pure Vibration. 1968
Vibration pure
Vibración Pura

Metal, wood, paint and nylon cord,
40¼ x 67¾ x 6⅜"

Lent by the artist

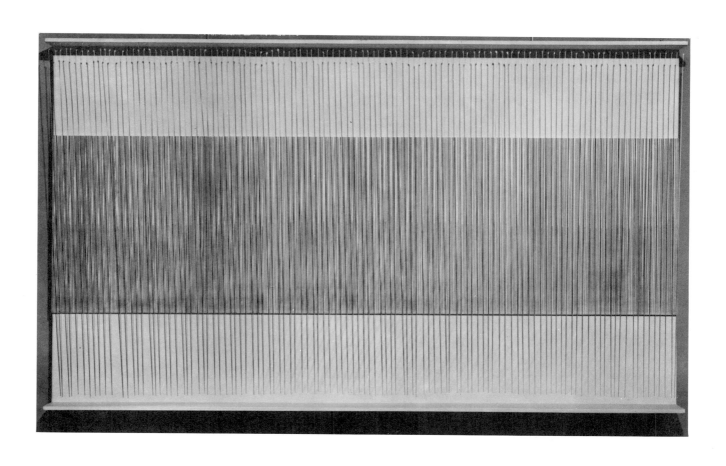

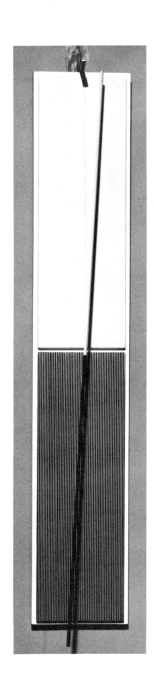

56
Red and White Vertical. 1968
Verticale rouge et blanche
Vertical Rojo y Blanco

Metal, wood, nylon cord and paint, 39½ x 6¾ x 5″

Lent by the artist

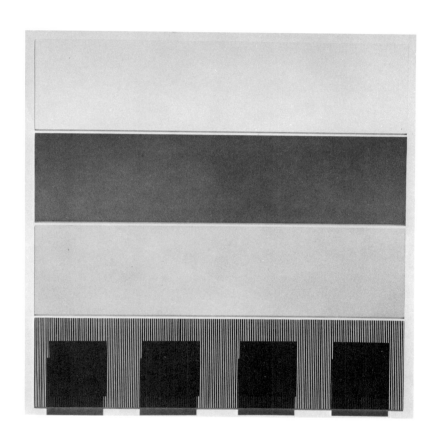

57
Four Squares with Blue Band. 1969
Quatre carrés à bande bleue
Quatros Cuadrados y Faja Azul
Wood and plaka, 43 x 41¾ x 6″
Collection William and Sylvia Ellis

58

Little Circle with Fine Black and Red Rods. 1969
Petit rond avec tiges fines noires et rouges
Circulo Pequeño con Varillas Finas Negras y Rojas

Metal, wood, nylon cord and paint, 11″ diameter x
4½″ deep

Lent by the artist

59
Suspended Volume with Metallic Rods. 1969
Volume suspendu avec tiges métalliques
Volumen Suspendido con Varillas Metálicas

Metal, wood, nylon cord and paint, 39½ ″ diameter x
11″ deep

Lent by the artist

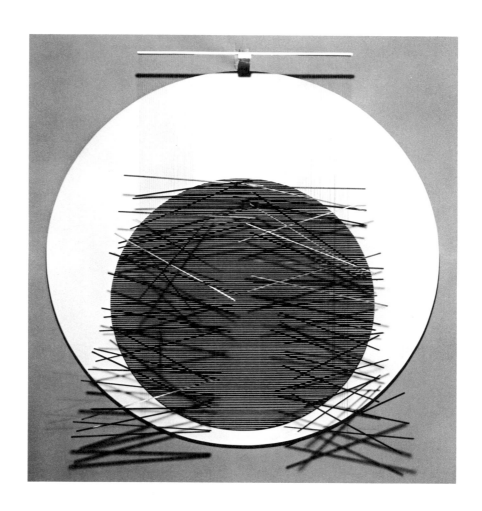

60
Red and Orange Progression. 1969
Progression rouge et orange
Progresión Rojay Anaranjado
Aluminum and paint, 98½ x 275⅝ x 55⅛″
Courtesy of Marlborough Gallery Inc., New York

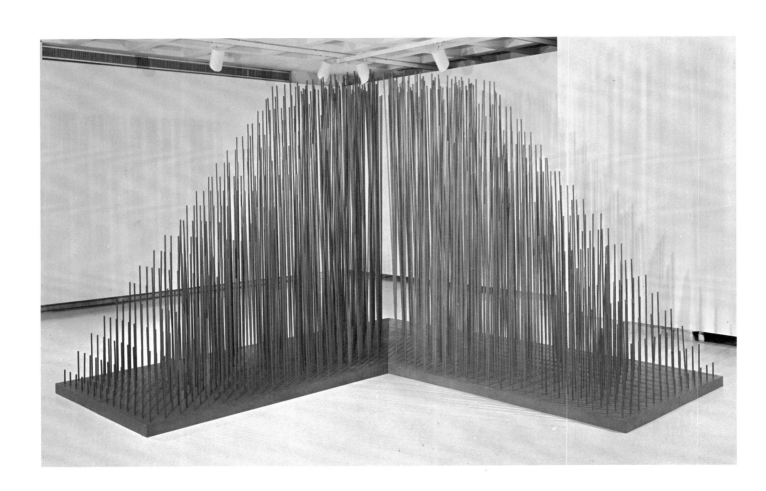

61
Cube with Ambiguous Space. 1969
Cube à espace ambigu
Cubo con Espacio Ambíguo

Plexiglas and paint, 88½ x 88½ x 88½ "
Lent by the artist

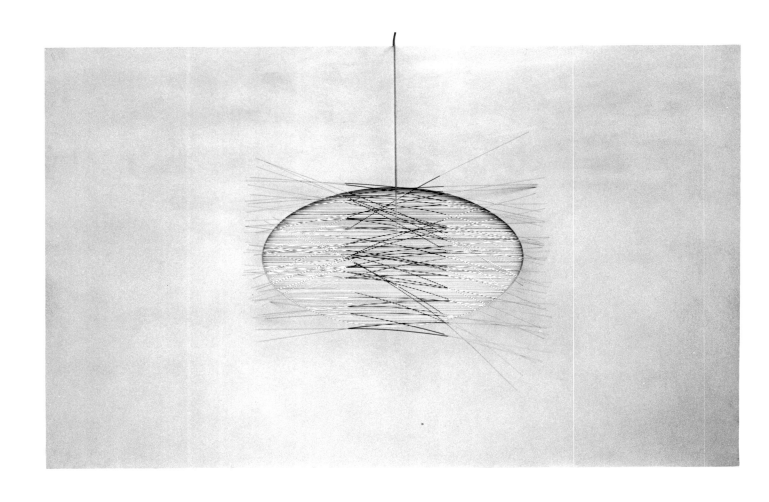

62
A Hole over Orange. 1970
Un Trou sur l'orange
Un Hueco sobre el Anaranjado
Metal painted relief, 59 x 95 x 11½"
Lent by Galerie Françoise Mayer, Brussels

63

Big Cadmium. 1970
Grand cadmium
Gran Cadmium

Wood, metal and plaka, 57 x 75 x 6″

Collection Museo de Arte Moderno ''Jesús Soto,''
Ciudad Bolivar, Venezuela

64
Black and Sikkens Mat 724. 1971
Noir et sikkens mat 724
Negro y Sikkens Mat 724

Metal, wood and paint, 45¼ x 59½ x 5″

Lent by the artist

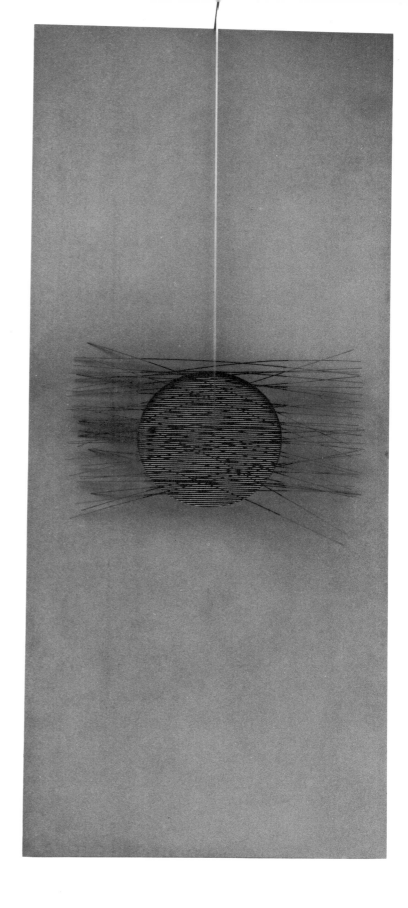

65
All Blue. 1971
Tout bleu
Todo Azul

Wood, wire, metal, paint and nylon cord,
94¾ x 39½ x 9⅝ ″
Lent by Galerie Denise René, Paris, New York

66
White and Pink T's. 1972
Tes blanches et roses
Tes Blancas y Rosas
Wood, plaka and metal, 39½ x 39½ x 4 ½ ″
Collection Alfredo and Yolanda Boulton

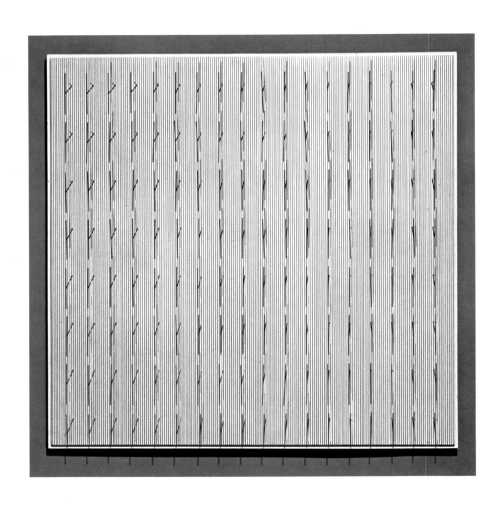

67
Green and Black T's. 1972
Tes vertes et noires
Tes Verdas y Negras
Wood, plaka and metal, 39½ x 39½ x 4½″
Collection Alfredo and Yolanda Boulton

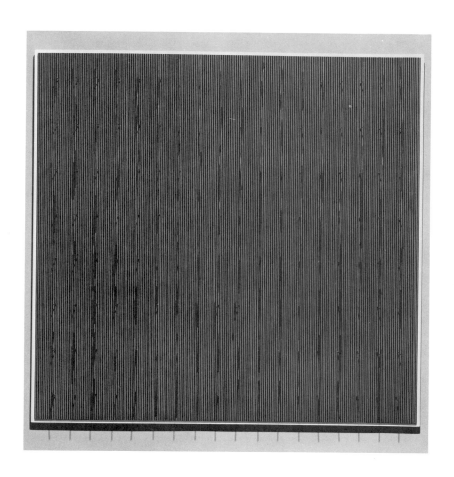

68
Ring. 1972
Anneau
Annillo
Metal, paint and nylon cord, 15½ x 19 x 13″
Collection Rosa Aguilera

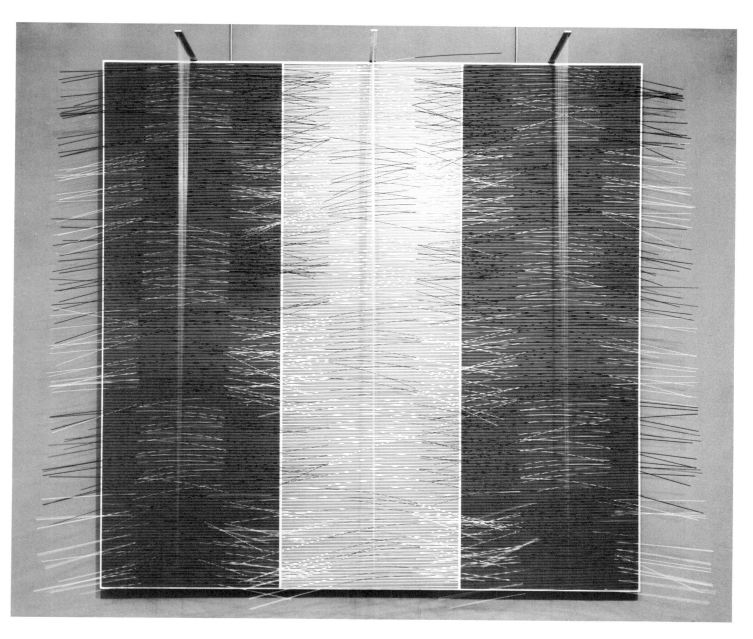

69
Black and White Triptych. 1973
Triptyque noir et blanc
Tríptico Negro y Blanco

Wood, wire, metal, paint and nylon cord,
79¾ x 86½ x 16½"

Lent by Galerie Denise René, Paris, New York

70
Pink Column. 1973
Colonne rose
Columna Rosa

Wood, wire, metal, paint and nylon cord,
84½ x 79¾ ″

Lent by Galerie Denise René, Paris, New York

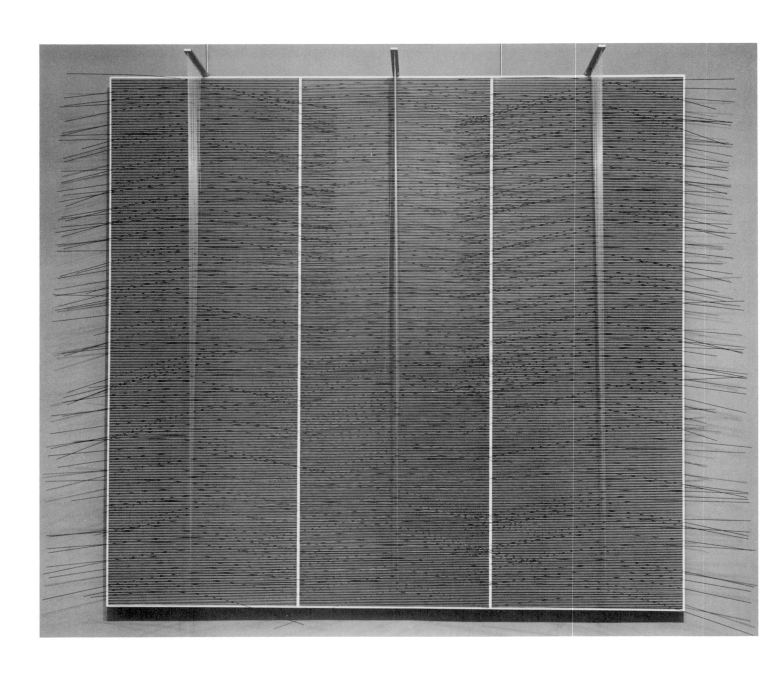

71
Diptych of T's over White and Black. 1974
Diptyque des tes sur blanc et noir
Díptico de Tes sobre Blanco y Negro

Wood, metal and paint, 79¾ x 88 x 6¾ ″

Lent by Galerie Denise René, Paris, New York

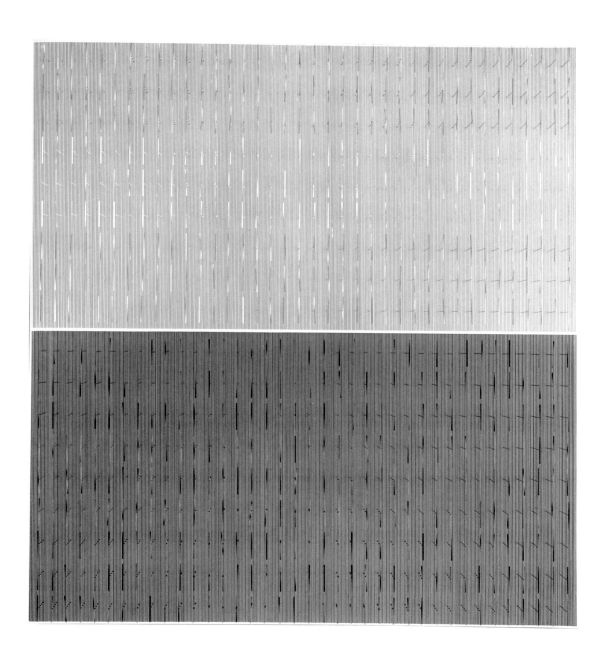

72
Approached Squares. 1974
Carrés rapprochés
Cuadrados a Cercados

Wood, metal and paint, 40½ x 40½ x 8″

Lent by Galerie Denise René, Paris, New York

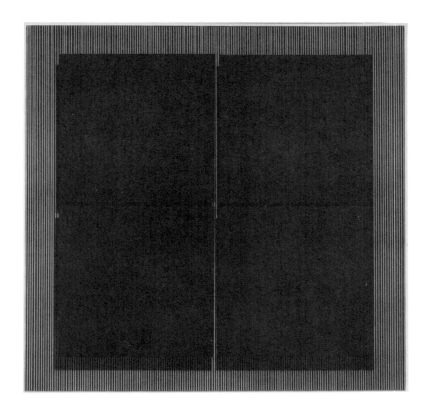

73
Big White. 1974
Grand blanc
Gran Blanco
Wood, metal and paint, 79¾ x 56 x 3″
Courtesy of the Renault Co.

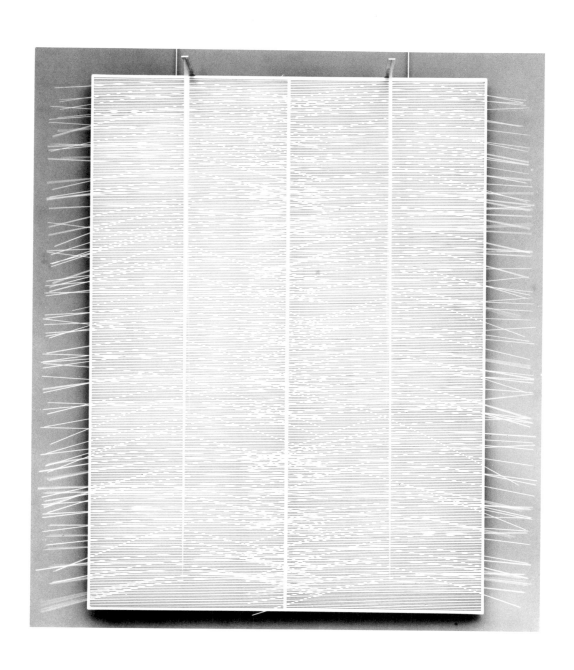

74
Big Yellow. 1974
Grand jaune
Gran Amarillo
Wood, wire, metal, paint and nylon cord,
79¾ x 56 x 16½ ″
Courtesy of the Renault Co.

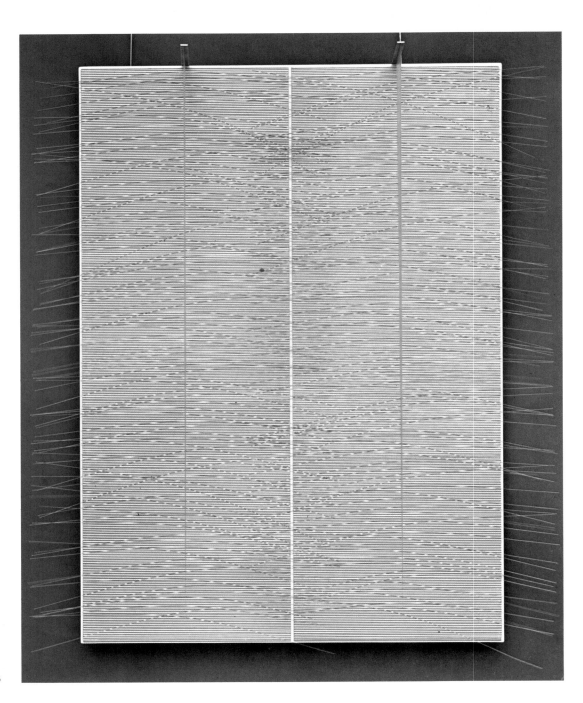

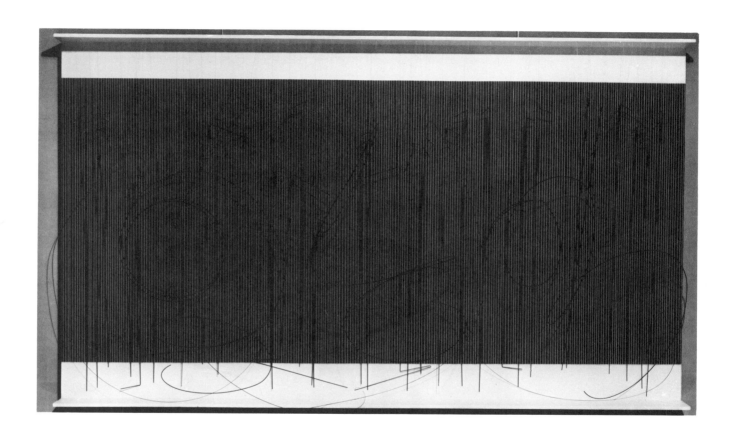

75
Spiral Writing. 1974
Ecriture spirale
Escritura Espiral

Wood, wire, paint and nylon cord, 40 x 67¾ x 7¼ ″
Courtesy of the Renault Co.

76
Watercolor. 1974
L'Aquarelle
La Acuarela
Wood, metal, paint and nylon cord, 44 x 79¾ x 6½"
Private Collection, Paris

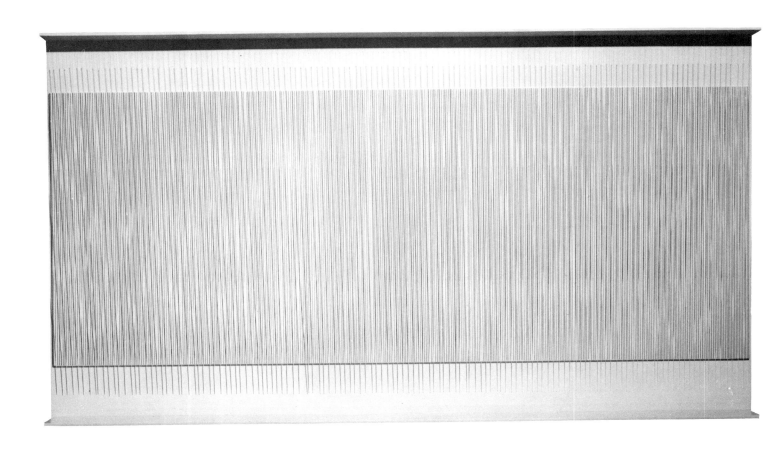

77
Fine Black Writing. 1974
Ecriture noire fine
Escritura Negra Fina

Wood, metal, paint and nylon cord, 40 x 67¾ x 6¼ ″
Courtesy of the Renault Co.

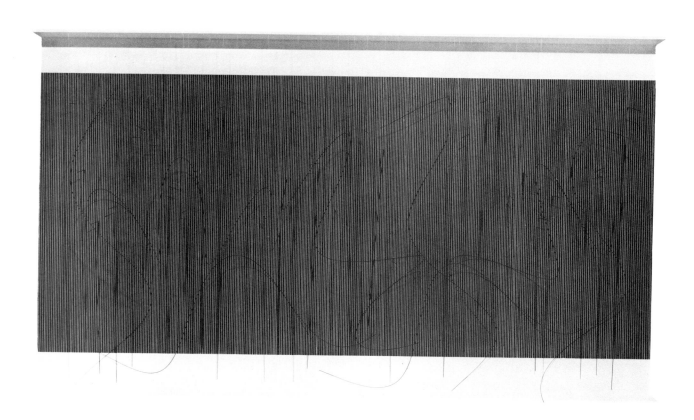

78
First White Writing. 1974
Première écriture blanche
Prima Escritura Blanca

Wood, metal, paint and nylon cord, 40 x 67¾ x 5″

Private Collection, Paris

79
Triptych with Violet. 1974
Triptyque avec du violet
Tríptico con Violeta

Wood, metal, paint and nylon cord,
79¾ x 83½ x 17½ "

Lent by Galerie Denise René, Paris, New York

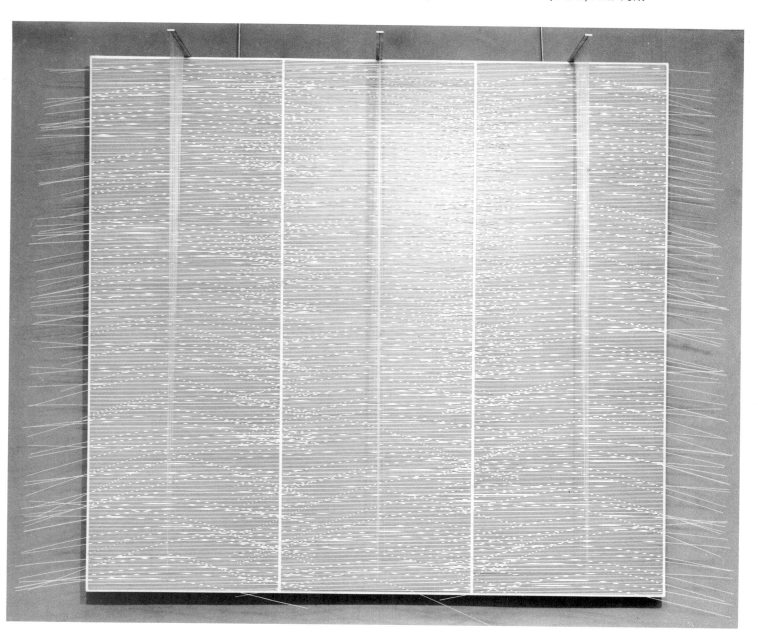

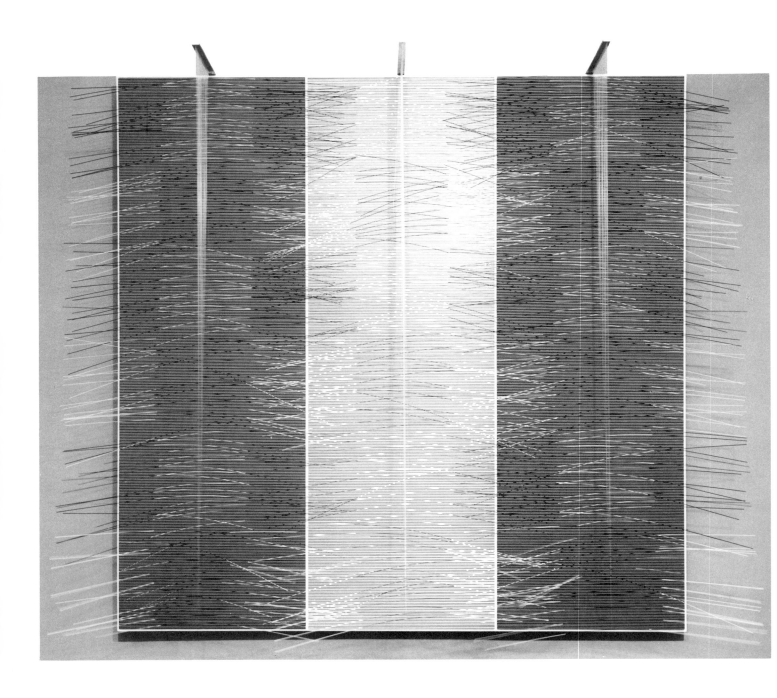

80
Triptych of Virtual Squares. 1974
Triptyque aux carrés virtuelles
Tríptico a Cuadrados Virtuales

Wood, metal, paint and nylon cord,
83¾ x 83¾ x 18″

Lent by Galerie Denise René, Paris, New York

81
Big Pink Wall. 1974
Grand mur rose
Gran Murale Rosa

Iron

Lent by the artist

Illustrated in catalogue supplement

82
Guggenheim Penetrable. 1974
Pénétrable Guggenheim
Penetrable Guggenheim

Lent by the artist

Illustrated in catalogue supplement

Chronology

1923
Born in Ciudad Bolivar, Venezuela.

1942-1947
Studied at Escuela de Artes Plásticas, Caracas.

1943-1949
Exhibited, Salón Oficial Anual de Arte Venezolano, Caracas.

1947-1950
Director of Escuela de Artes Plásticas, Maracaibo, Venezuela.

1949
First one man show, Taller Libre de Arte, Caracas.

1950
Moved to Paris, where he still lives and works.
Interest in Mondrian, Malevich and Bauhaus.

1951
Exhibited, Salon des Réalités Nouvelles, Paris.
First works composed entirely of single, systematically repeated forms.

1952
Began to make works in series.

1953
First use of plexiglas.
Important step towards development of Kineticism in creation of a work with two layers of plexiglas covered with dots which seemed to move as the spectator moved.

1954
Soto, Agam and Tinguely formulated concepts of Kineticism.

1955-1957
Further development of kinetic concepts in structures of geometric elements: constructions of two, three or four planes with spirals or stripes which seem to move as the viewer moves.

1957
Grillworks, twisted wires forming irregular geometric constructions on rough polyester and stucco surfaces replace plexiglas.

1958
Vibrations series: introduction of hanging elements which move.
Two kinetic murals and a sculpture for the Venezuelan Pavilion at Exposition Internationale, Brussels. Sculpture for the garden of Escuela d'Architettura, Caracas.

1960
Premio Nacional de Pintura, Museo de Bellas Artes, Caracas.

1963
Wolf Prize, São Paulo Bienal.

1964
David Bright Prize, Venice Biennale.

1965
First one man show in New York, Kootz Gallery.

1966
Panoramic vibrating wall for Venice Biennale.

1967
Kinetic sculptures for Venezuelan Pavilion, *Expo 67,* Montreal.

1968
Two walls and a sculpture at main entrance of the Faculté de Médecine et de Pharmacie, Rennes.

1969
Began *Extensions:* expanses filled with rods extending upward.
Culmination of attempts to integrate the spectator into the work of art with the creation of *Penetrables,* rains of hanging nylon threads through which the viewer walks.

1970
Mural for UNESCO building, Paris.

1971
Retrospective, Museo de Bellas Artes, Caracas.

1973
Model for his Kinetic Environment for the new Renault Factory, Billancourt, Paris.

One Man Exhibitions and Reviews

Taller Libre de Arte, Caracas, May 29 - June 5, 1949.

Galerie Denise René, Paris, March 9-31, 1956, *Soto Kinetic Structures.*

Galerie Aujourd'hui, Palais des Beaux-Arts, Brussels, January 26 - February 13, 1957, *Peintures Cinétiques de Soto.* Catalogue with text by Guillermo Meneses.

Museo de Bellas Artes, Caracas, opened June 30, 1957, *Soto. Estructuras Cinéticas.*

Galerie Iris Clert, Paris, 1959.

Galerie Rudolf Zwirner, Essen, 1961. Traveled to Galerie Brusberg, Hanover, March 15 - April 30, 1961.

Museo de Bellas Artes, Caracas, April-May 1961, *Vibraciones. Soto.*

Galerie Ad Libitum, Antwerp/Anvers, February 2 - March 15, 1962, *J. R. Soto, Vibrations 1958-1962.*

Galerie Edouard Loeb, Paris, June 5 - July 13, 1962.

Museum Haus Lange, Krefeld, Germany, November-December 1963, *Soto, Tableaux Cinétiques.* Catalogue with text by Paul Wember.

Galerie Müller, Stuttgart, January 25 - February 28, 1964, *Jesús Raphael Soto.* Catalogue with text by Paul Wember.

Museo de Bellas Artes, Caracas, November 1964, *Jesús Soto. Pintura.*

Kootz Gallery, New York, March 9-27, 1965, *Vibrations by Soto.* Catalogue with text by Umbro Apollonio.

Rosenthal, Nan, "New York: Gallery Notes," *Art in America,* vol. 53, no. 1, February 1965, p. 116.

Berkson, William, "In the Galleries," *Arts Magazine,* vol. 39, no. 9, May 1965, p. 68.

Galerie Edouard Loeb, Paris, June 1 - July 31, 1965, *Soto.*

Watt, Alexander, "Exhibition at the Galerie Edouard Loeb," *Studio International,* vol. 170, no. 869, September 1965, p. 127.

Signals Gallery, London, October 14 - December 24, 1965, *J. R. Soto: His Ideas, His Work, His Achievements.* Catalogue with texts by Umbro Apollonio, Guy Brett, Jean Clay.

Celant, Germano, "Achievements of J. R. Soto 1950-1965, Fifteen Years of Vibrations," *Casabella,* no. 301, January 1966, pp. 67-68.

Burn, Guy, "Carta de Londres: Retrospectiva de 1965," *Goya,* no. 73, July-August 1966, pp. 42-47.

Galerie Schmela, Dusseldorf, opened February 2, 1966. Traveled to Pfalzgalerie des Bezirksverbandes, Kaiserslautern, Germany, June 23-July 24, 1966.

Galleria del Naviglio, Milan, February 24 - March 9, 1966, *Soto.* Catalogue with text by Umbro Apollonio.

Galleria del Deposito, Genoa, opened February 25, 1966, *Jesús Rafael Soto.* Catalogue with text by Germano Celant.

Kootz Gallery, New York, March 1-19, 1966.

Piene, Nan R., "Exhibition at the Kootz Gallery," *Art in America,* vol. 54, no. 1, January - February 1966, p. 120.

R [osenstein], H [arris], "Exhibition at Kootz Gallery," *Art News,* vol. 65, no. 1, March 1966, p. 64.

Goldin, Amy, "In the Galleries," *Arts Magazine,* vol. 40, no. 7, May 1966, p. 67.

Galleria del Cavallino, Venice, March 23 - April 4, 1966, *Soto.* Catalogue with text by Umbro Apollonio.

XXXIII Biennale Internazionale d'Arte, Venice, June 18 - October 16, 1966, *Jesús R. Soto.*

Alvard, J., "La XXXIIIe Biennale de Venise," *Aujourd'hui,* no. 54, September 1966, p. 100.

Centro Arte Viva, Trieste, 1966.

Galerie Denise René, Paris, May - June 1967, *De L'Art optique à l'art cinétique.* Catalogue with text by Jean Clay.

Museo de Bellas Artes, Caracas, July 1967, *Jesús Soto. Obras Recientes.*

Ramos, Giugni Angel, "Soto en el Museo Nacional," *Zona Franca,* no. 48, August 1967, p. 58.

Expo 67, Venezuelan Pavilion, Montreal, 1967, *Soto: l'Effet-Moiré.* Catalogue with text by Alfredo Boulton.

Galerie Françoise Mayer, Brussels, February - March 1968.

Kunsthalle, Bern, May 21 - June 30, 1968, *Die Acht Seligkeiten des Jesús Raphael Soto.* Catalogue with text by Paul Wember, "Dialoog J. R. Soto," (dated April 1965) by Guy Brett. Traveled to Kestner Gesellschaft, Hanover, July 24 - September 8, 1968; Kunstverein für die Rheinlande und Westfalen, Dusseldorf, October 8 - November 10, 1968. Catalogue with text by Karl-Heinz Hering, *J. R. Soto;* Stedelijk Museum, Amsterdam, January 11 - February 23, 1969, *Soto Itinéraire 1950-1968.* Catalogue with text by Jean Clay; Palais des Beaux-Arts, Brussels, March 6 - April 4, 1969; Musée d'Art Moderne de la Ville de Paris, Paris, June 10 - August 21, 1969, *Soto.* Catalogue with text by Jean Clay.

Ammann, J. C., "Jesús Raphael Soto oder die Visualisierung der Raum-Zeitmaterie-Trinitat (Kunsthalle, Bern)," *Art International,* vol. 7, no. 8, October 1968, p. 55.

"Exhibition Kunsthalle, Bern," *Werk,* vol. 55, no. 7, July 1968, pp. 487-489.

"La Trinità di Soto," *Domus,* no. 473, April 4, 1969, pp. 48-51.

Clay, Jean, "Soto en Amsterdam," *Revista Nacional de Cultura,* no. 187, February-March 1969, pp. 92-101.

Michel, Jacques, "Le Cinétisme au musée l'autre nature de Soto," *Le Monde,* June 26, 1969, p. 17.

Peppiatt, M. "Exhibition at Musée d'Art Moderne," *Art International,* vol. 13, no. 75, September 1969, p. 5.

Gállego, Julián, "Crónica de Paris. Soto, la Joven Escultura y la Vieja Arquitectura," *Goya,* no. 92, September-October 1969, pp. 97-98.

Marlborough Galleria d'Arte, Rome, opened May 28, 1968.

Galleria Lorenzelli, Bergamo, Italy, December 1968 - January 1969, *J. R. Soto.* Catalogue with texts by Marco Valsecchi, Umbro Apollonio, Jean Clay.

Galleria Notizie, Turin, January 22-February 28, 1969, *Soto*. Catalogue with text by Jean Clay.

Galleria del Naviglio, Milan, March 26-April 9, 1969.

Svensk-Franska Kunstgalleriet, Stockholm, opened September 26, 1969. Catalogue with text.

Marlborough-Gerson Gallery, Inc., New York, October-November, 1969, *Soto*. Catalogue with text by Guy Brett.

"Exposición de Soto en la Galleria Marlborough," *El Nacional,* October 24, 1969.

Imber, Sofia, "Soto en Nueva York," *Bohemia,* no. 346, November 16, 1969, pp. 12-17.

Edgar, Natalie, "Exhibition at Marlborough-Gerson Gallery," *Art News,* vol. 68, no. 8, December 1969, p. 71.

Estudio Actual, Caracas, 1969.

Galleria Giraldi, Leghorn, Italy, 1969.

Galleria Flori, Florence, 1969.

Galerie Bonnier, Geneva, opened January 15, 1970.

Kunstverein, Mannheim, 1970. Traveled to Pflaz-galerie des Bezirksverbandes, Kaiserslautern, Germany, May 31-June 28, 1970; Ulmer Museum, Ulm, Germany, July 12-September 6, 1970, *Jesús Raphael Soto*. Catalogue with text by Eva Fehsenbecker.

Brackert, Gisela, "Kunstverein, Mannheimer," *Das Kunstwerk,* vol. 23, no. 9-10, June 1970, pp. 79-80.

Galerie Denise René, Paris, June-July 1970.

Galerie Buchholz, Munich, September 22-October 31, 1970, *Soto*. Catalogue with text.

Galerie Suvremene, Zagreb, 1970.

Galerie Semiha Huber, Zurich, 1970.

Galerie Godart Leffort, Montreal, 1970.

Allegre, Christian, "Soto à la Galerie Godard-Lefort," *Le Devoir,* March 21, 1970.

Galeria de la Nova Loggia, Bologna, 1970.

Museum of Contemporary Art, Chicago, February 13-March 28, 1971. Traveled to Akron Art Center, Ohio, April 7-May 9, 1971.

"Gran Exposición de Jesús Soto en Museo de Arte Moderno de Chicago," *El Nacional,* May 26, 1970.

Museo de Bellas Artes, Caracas, July-August 1971, *Soto: Retrospectiva.* Catalogue with texts by Guillermo Meneses and Alfredo Boulton. Traveled to Museo de Arte Moderno, Bogota, February 10-March 31, 1972.

"Soto Retrospective in Caracas," *Art News,* vol. 70, no. 7, November 1971, p. 6.

"La Retrospectiva de Soto," *El Nacional,* Caracas, July 24, 1971, p. D-11.

J. H. B., "La Retrospectiva Soto," *El Nacional,* Caracas, July 25, 1971.

"La Exposición de Soto: Cultura a Cambio de Balas," *El Tiempo,* January 26, 1972, p. 12-A.

Garzon, Miguel Antonio, "Arte Venezolano Exponen en Bogota," *El Espectador,* January 30, 1972.

Boulton, Alfredo, "Plastica del Movimento," *Magazine Dominical,* January 30, 1972, pp. 2-3.

"Jesús Soto: Mis Obras no Tienen Fronteras," *El Siglo,* February 2, 1972, p. 8.

Solvente, Camilo, "A la Espera de Soto," *El Tiempo,* February 5, 1972.

Garzon, Miguel Antonio, "Exposición de Soto el 10," *El Espectador,* February 6, 1972, p. 6-B.

Martha Jackson Gallery, New York, September 28-October 16, 1971.

E [dgar], N [atalie], "Jackson Gallery," *Art News,* vol. 70, no. 7, November 1971, p. 82.

Green, Denise, "New York Gallery Reviews," *Arts Magazine,* vol. 46, no. 2, November 1971, pp. 62-63.

Galerie Denise René-Hans Meyer, Dusseldorf, 1971.

Kunstverein, Kaiserslautern, Germany, 1971.

Galleria Rotta, Milan, April-May 1971.

"Mostre d'Arte," *Corriere Della Sera,* May 7, 1971.

Galerie Beyeler, Basel, April 20-May 1972. Traveled to Galerie Alice Pauli, Lausanne, June 17-July 31, 1972; Galleria Levi, Milan, Fall, 1972.

Schurr, Gérald, "Galerie Beyeler; exhibit," *Connoisseur,* vol. 179, no. 722, April 1972, p. 295.

Estudio Actual, Caracas, 1972.

Formes et Muraux, Lyon, 1972.

Galleria Corsini, Rome, opened February 18, 1973.

Universidad Central de Venezuela, Caracas, 1973.

Estudio Dos, Valencia, Venezuela, 1973.

Fermin, Alfredo, "Soto, el Universal: El Arte Debe, Salir a la Calle y Convertirse en Manifestación Colectiva," *El Carabobeno,* March 31, 1973. p. 5.

Arte/Contacto, Caracas, opened March 18, 1973. Catalogue with text.

Gàleria Godel, Rome. 1973.

131

Bibliography

BOOKS
One-man exhibition catalogues are included in the exhibitions list.

Bann, S., Gadney, R., Popper, F. and Steadman, P., *Four Essays on Kinetic Art,* London, 1966, pp. 6, 37, 49, 57-59, illus.

Catlin, Stanton Loomis and Grieder, Terence, *Art of Latin America since Independence,* New Haven, 1966, pp. 125, 197, 238.

Pellegrini, Aldo, *New Tendencies in Art,* New York, 1966, pp. 163, 166, 169, 173.

Messer, Thomas, M., *The Emergent Decade,* The Guggenheim Museum, New York, 1966, pp. 137-143, illus.

Compton, Michael, *Optical and Kinetic Art,* Tate Gallery, London, 1967.

"Jesús Soto," *Instituto Nacional de Cultura y Bellas Artes,* Caracas, 1967, pp. 5-22.

Rickey, George, *Constructivism, Origins and Evolution,* New York, 1967, pp. 62, 126, 189, 196.

Popper, Frank, *Origins and Development of Kinetic Art,* Greenwich, 1968, pp. 106-108, 204-205, 220, 238, 240.

Fujieda, Teruo, ed., *Art Now—Form and Structure,* Japan, 1971, pp. 100-101. Text in Japanese.

Boulton, Alfredo, *Soto,* Caracas, 1973.

PERIODICALS
One-man exhibition reviews are included in the exhibition list under the appropriate show.

Erminy, Perán, "La Plástica Cinemática de Jesús Soto," *Integral,* no. 8, August 1957.

Diament de Sujo, Clara, "Pintores Venezolanos: Soto," *Revista Shell,* December 1957, pp. 19-24.

Meneses, Guillermo, "Soto," *El Farol,* no. 191, November-December, 1960, pp. 29-35.

Schneider, Pierre, "Fed-up Art in Paris," *Art News,* vol. 59, no. 10, February 1961, p. 50.

Valladares, F., "Vibraciónes de Soto," *Punto,* no. 3, July 1961.

Navarro, Luis, "Pintura y Escultura en la Ciudad Universitaria," *Revista Shell,* no. 41, December 1961, p. 28.

Habasque, Guy, "La XXXIe Biennale de Venise," *L'Oeil,* no. 93, September 1962, pp. 41, 73.

Jürgen-Fischer, K., "XXXIe Biennale, Venedig," *Das Kunstwerk,* vol. 16, no. 3, September 1962, p. 4.

França, J. A., "Les Expositions à Paris," *Aujourd'hui,* no. 38, September 1962, p. 53.

"VII Bienal de Arte de São Paulo," *Habitat,* vol. 13, no. 74, December 1963, pp. 64, 93.

D.I.M., "De Soto la Nature Recréée," *Arts, Lettres, Spectacles, Musique,* no. 951, February 26 - March 3, 1964, p. 13.

Diament de Sujo, Clara, "De Estos 25 Años . . . (La distancia de dos salones de pintura venezolana)," *El Farol,* no. 209, April-June 1964, p. 26.

Bayl, Friedrich, "25 Salón Nacional de Caracas," *Goya,* no. 61, July-August 1964,, pp. 51-53.

Raymont, Henry, "City in Argentina Boasts Big Art Show," *New York Times,* October 11, 1964.

Coplans, John, "West Coast Notes," *Art International,* vol. 9, no. 1, February 1965, p. 48.

Meneses, Sofia, "Jesús Soto: Creador Infatigable y Artista Universal," *Revista Diners',* no. 3, June 1965.

"Soto Voce Ad Infinitum," *The Observer,* March 21, 1965.

Picard, Lil, "Op-report," *Das Kunstwerk,* vol. 19, no. 1, July 1965, pp. 8-11.

Brett, Guy, "Pure Relations—The Art of Jesús Raphael Soto," *Art International,* vol. 9, no. 7, October 1965, pp. 17-21, illus.

Russell, John, "Inward Energies," *The Sunday Times,* November 11, 1965.

Gosling, Nigel, "Cairo to Caro," *The Observer,* November 7, 1965.

Trajtenberg, Mario, "Vibrations from Venezuela," *The Guardian,* November 9, 1965.

Lynton, Norbert, "Soto and Gilbert Exhibitions," *The Guardian,* November 19, 1965.

Cutler, Carol, "Paris: the No-color Look," *Art in America,* vol. 53, no. 6, December 1965, p. 105.

"Revolucionario Del Arte," *Life,* 1965-1966, pp. V116-V122. Spanish edition.

Clay, Jean, "J. R. Soto: Creating 'Imaginary Space'," *Studio International,* vol. 171, no. 873, January 1966, pp. 2-5.

Ernest, John, "Constructivism and Content," *Studio International,* vol. 171, no. 876, April 1966, p. 155.

Freudenheim, T. L., "Kinetic Art," *Albright Knox Gallery Notes,* vol. 29, no. 2, 1966, p. 8.

Menna, Filiberto, "Jesús Rafael Soto," *Marcatre,* nos. 26-29, December 1966 - March 1967, pp. 158-159.

Clay, Jean, "Salon des Réalités Nouvelles," *Studio International,* vol. 173, no. 885, January 1967, pp. 44-47.

"Statements by Kinetic Artists," *Studio International,* vol. 173, no. 886, February 1967, p. 60.

Popper, Frank, "Soto: l'effet moiré," *Naissance de l'art cinétique/L'image du mouvement dans les arts plastiques depuis 1860,* 1967, pp. 100-102.

Soto, Jesús, "Soto Habla de Jesús Soto," *Imagen,* no. 3, June 1967, pp. 9-16.

Guevara, Roberto, "Soto y la Visión Transformante," *Imagen,* no. 5, July 1967, p. 24.

Pineda, Rafael, "Hasta Soto," *El Minero,* vol. 7, no. 11, September 1967.

Henault, Gilles, "L'Art en mouvement et le mouvement dans l'art," *Vie des Arts,* no. 49, Winter 1967-1968, pp. 22-26.

DuParc, Christiane, "Les Sud-Américains ont pris Paris," *Le Nouvel Adam,* no. 19, February 1968, p. 49.

Clay, Jean, "Los Penetrables de Soto," *Imagen,* no. 34, October 1968, pp. 18-19.

Comte, Phillippe, "Soto dans le labyrinthe," *Opus International,* no. 12, June 1969, pp. 27-29.

Hahn, Otto, "Soto veut être regardé de l'interieur," *L'Expres,* June 16-22, 1969.

Cutler, Carol, "Art in Paris: Sheltered in a Fringed Plastic Haven," *Herald Tribune,* June 21-22, 1969.

Clay, Jean, "Soto," *Connaissance des Arts,* no. 208, June 1969, pp. 80-83.

Granados, Valdes A., "Entrevista con Jesús Soto," *Punto,* no. 38, June 1969, pp. 60-64.

Kramer, Hilton, "Victims of a Fatal Quality of Parisian Chic," *The New York Times,* July 13, 1969.

DuParc, Christiane, "Le Descartes du cinétisme," *Le Nouvel Observateur,* no. 244, July 14, 1969, p. 36.

Batallan, Lorenzo, "La Importancia Internacional de Soto," *El Nacional,* July 30, 1969, p. 10.

Gállego, Julián, "Crónica de Paris," *Goya,* no. 91, July-August 1969, pp. 34-35.

Clay, Jean, "Soto's Penetrables," *Studio International,* vol. 178, no. 914, September 1969, pp. 75-77.

Guevara, Roberto, "Arte lo Nuevo de Ver: Soto 1969. Nuevas Experiencias en la Lectura de la Realidad," *Punto,* no. 39, September 1969, pp. 61-63.

Vives, Teresa Piñana, "Exonerar de Impuestos Al Arte, Propone Sofia Imber," *El Mundo,* October 30, 1969, p. 5.

"Casi Dos Metros Cubicos Mide Penetrable de Soto," *El Nacional,* October 30, 1969.

J.H.R., "Neue Kinetische Abstraktionen," *Aufbau,* November 7, 1969, p. 18.

Andreae, Christopher, "Soto," *The Christian Science Monitor,* December 8, 1969, p. 8.

Montero Castro, Roberto, "Visión Actual de Soto," *Imagen,* no. 40, 1969, p. 22.

Stellweg, Carla, "Jesús Soto y los Penetrables," *Excelsior,* January 11, 1970.

D'Elme, Patrick, "La Logique de Soto," *Cimaise,* no. 97, May-August 1970, pp. 12-23.

Glusberg, Jorge, "Il Bienal de Arte Coltejer de Medellin," *Goya,* no. 97, July-August 1970, p. 38.

Johnson, Elaine, L., "A Report on the 'Primera Bienal del Grabado Latinoamericano' in San Juan de Puerto Rico," *Artist's Proof,* vol. 10, 1970, p. 101.

Johnson, Elaine, L., "Young Printmakers in Latin America," *Art in America,* vol. 59, no. 1, January 1971, p. 116.

Vestrini, Miyó, "Las Obras Que Integraran Exposición de Jesús Soto Seran Elaboradas en Venezuela," *El Nacional,* February 17, 1971.

Rondón, Lossada, J., "Trabajará Jésus Soto," *El Nacional,* March 27, 1971, p. C-4.

Giugni, Angel Ramos, "La Impresionante Obra de Soto," *Imagen,* no. 5, July 1971, pp. 1-5, 23-30.

Vestrini, Miyó, "Jesús Soto: Venezuela es Uno de los Raros Paises de América Latina Donde Existe la Necesidad de Crear un Arte Nuevo," *El Nacional,* July 24, 1971, p. ARTEC-8.

Briceño, José Hernán, "Atraidos por la Obra de Soto," *El Nacional,* July 26, 1971, p. C-11.

Carpio, Oscar, "Marceau y Soto, O Bip y el Arte Cinetico," *Punto,* Septèmber-October 1971, pp. 53-57.

"Exhibit of Constructions Opens Today at IU," *Herald Times,* Bloomington, Indiana, November 7, 1971.

Barron, Amalia, "Como Vive Jesús Soto," *Vanidades,* vol. 12, no. 14, July 10, 1972, pp. 24-29.

Greenwood, M., "Soto, Thépot, Calleja, Hayden," *Arts Canada,* no. 29, Autumn 1972, pp. 104-105.

"Entrevista con Jesús Rafael Soto," *Boletin Sandoz,* no. 26, 1972, pp. 15-28.

Alvarenga, Teresa, "Soto en Ciudad Bolivar: Estos no es un Museo Sino un Centro de Investigación de la Plastica Experimental," *El Nacional,* August 25, 1973, pp. ARTEC.

Batallán, Lorenzo, "En un Penetrable Libro Optico Alfredo Boulton Presenta: Soto," *El Nacional,* November 21, 1973.

Pineda, Rafael, "Soto en el Contexto del Cinetismo," *El Universal,* January 9, 1974.

FILMS ON SOTO

1958   Angel Hurtado, "Vibrations," Paris.

1962   Angel Hurtado, "Vibrationsoto," Caracas.
Angel Hurtado and Clara Diament de Sujo, "Asi nace un Mural," Caracas.

1963   Film for Belgian television.

1964   "Mobile Sculpture at the Lamda Theatre," by Soto, Takis and Pol Bury.
"Kinetic Art, Works of Soto, Camargo and Takis," BBC TV 1 London.

1965   "Soto at Signals," BBC TV 2 London.

1967   Jean-Jacques Copetta, "Soto," Paris.

1968   Vittorio Armentano, "Soto," Rome.
Croce, "Soto," Paris.

1969   Kunsthalle Nuremberg, "Soto," for television.

1972   Alfredo Brandler, "Soto ou la volonté," Caracas.

1973   Angel Hurtado, "Soto."

Photographic Credits

Exhibition 74/6

6,000 copies of this catalogue designed by Malcolm Grear
Designers have been typeset by Dumar Typesetting, Inc. and
printed by The Meriden Gravure Company in November 1974 for
the Trustees of The Solomon R. Guggenheim Foundation on
the occasion of
Soto: A Retrospective Exhibition